Summer Bridge Reading
Grades 4–5

Editor: Julie Kirsch

Layout Design: Tiara Reynolds

Inside Illustrations: Magen Mitchell

Cover Design: Chasity Rice

Cover Illustration: Wayne Miller

Printed in the USA • All rights reserved.   ISBN 978-1-60022-447-8

Table of Contents

The *Summer Bridge Reading* series is designed to help children improve their reading skills during the summer months and between grades. *Summer Bridge Reading* includes several extra components to help make your child's study of reading easier and more inviting.

For example, an **Assessment** test has been included to help you determine your child's reading knowledge and what skills need improvement. Use this test, as well as the **Assessment Analysis**, as a diagnostic tool for those areas in which your child may need extra practice.

Furthermore, the **Incentive Contract** will motivate your child to complete the work in *Summer Bridge Reading*. Together, you and your child choose the reward for completing specific sections of the book. Check off the pages that your child has completed, and he or she will have a record of his or her accomplishment.

Examples are included for each new skill that your child will learn. The examples are located in blue boxes at the top of the pages. Clear directions explain how to complete each activity.

Summer Reading List

Anderson, Laurie Halse

Fever 1793

Avi

The True Confessions of Charlotte Doyle

Balliett, Blue

Chasing Vermeer

Barry, Dave and Ridley Pearson

Peter and the Starcatchers

Bellairs, John

The Curse of the Blue Figurine

Berger, Melvin and Gilda Berger

The Real Vikings: Craftsmen, Traders, and Fearsome Raiders

Cassedy, Sylvia

Behind the Attic Wall

Collier, James Lincoln and Christopher Collier

My Brother Sam Is Dead

Conrad, Pam

My Daniel

Cooper, Susan

The Dark Is Rising series

Creech, Sharon

Chasing Redbird

Dahl, Roald

The Witches

DuPrau, Jeanne

The City of Ember

Erdrich, Louise

The Birchbark House

Farley, Walter

The Black Stallion

Frank, Anne

Anne Frank: The Diary of a Young Girl

George, Jean Craighead

My Side of the Mountain; Julie of the Wolves

Gray, Elizabeth Janet

Adam of the Road

Hautzig, Esther

The Endless Steppe

Irving, Washington

The Legend of Sleepy Hollow

Konigsburg, E. L.

From the Mixed-Up Files of Mrs. Basil E. Frankweiler

Lewis, C. S.

The Chronicles of Narnia series

Lord, Bette Bao

In the Year of the Boar and Jackie Robinson

McKinley, Robin

The Door in the Hedge; The Hero and the Crown

Naylor, Phyllis Reynolds

Shiloh

O'Dell, Scott

Island of the Blue Dolphins

Sachar, Louis

Holes

Speare, Elizabeth George

Calico Captive

Stanley, Diane

Michelangelo

Raskin, Ellen

The Westing Game

White, E. B.

Stuart Little

Winthrop, Elizabeth

The Castle in the Attic

Yep, Laurence

The Tiger's Apprentice

Summer Bridge Reading RB-904095

Incentive Contract

List your agreed-upon incentive for each section below. Place an *X* after each completed exercise.

	Activity Title	X	My Incentive Is:
9	Puzzling Words		
11	Which One?		
12	Word Relationships		
13	Amazing Analogies		
14	Analogies		
15	Elephants		
16	Check the Meaning		
17	Multiple Meanings		
18	From the Beginning		
19	Base Changes		
20	Comparisons		
21	What Does It Mean?		
22	What a Character!		
23	The Anasazi		
25	Freddie's New Home		

	Activity Title	X	My Incentive Is:
26	Space Exploration		
28	You Have the Idea!		
29	Writing a Main Idea		
30	Caring for the Environment		
31	Shiloh		
32	Wonton Soup		
33	Sod Houses		
35	Ty Cobb		
37	Questions and Answers		
38	Frosty		
39	Becoming Good Neighbors		
40	The Supreme Court		
42	Chart Facts		
44	In the Right Direction		
45	Figuring It Out		

	Activity Title	X	My Incentive Is:
46	That's Nonsense!		
48	Common Ground		
49	It's Not Like the Rest		
50	Ships of the Desert		
51	Winter Is a White Owl		
53	Finding the Cause		
54	It's a Match!		
55	That's a Fact!		
56	Endangered Environments		
57	You Decide		
58	Listening to Music		
60	The Riverdale Patriots		
62	Sailing in a Storm		
64	Accessories		
65	Occupations		

	Activity Title	X	My Incentive Is:
66	Frozen in Time		
68	Emilio's Tadpoles		
70	A Surprise for Krysia		
74	The Case of the Missing Heirloom		
79	Find Abe!		
81	Javier's Bike		
83	The Daring Young Man in the Vin Fiz		
85	The Lair of the High Cave Dragon		
87	From A to Z		
88	Using the Keys		
89	Encyclopedias		
90	Map It Out		
91	Staying on Topic		
92	Looking It Up		
93	Where Would You Look?		

Assessment Test

Read the passage below and answer questions 1–7.

A library is a treasure chest. Both libraries and treasure chests hold valuable riches. A treasure chest holds items of great monetary value, while a library contains items of great literary value. Open a treasure chest and you may discover one million dollars tucked inside. Enter a library and you will be transported to one of a million worlds hidden within the books.

Spending time in a library may be more valuable than spending a treasure. After money is spent, it is gone forever, but the wealth of knowledge and pleasure found in reading a good book stays with you for a lifetime.

Remember, a bird in the hand is worth two in the bush. Since the odds of finding a treasure chest full of gold in your neighborhood are not likely, you should search for a different kind of treasure. Find a library and start gathering the riches!

1. Write the two words in the third sentence that are synonyms.

   _____ and _____

2. Add a prefix to the word *likely* to make its definition change to *not likely*. _____

3. Write a homophone for the word *one*. _____

   Write a definition for *one* and its homophone. _____

   _____

4. Write the sentence that is a metaphor. _____

   _____

5. Underline the idiom in the third paragraph. What do you think it means?

   _____

   _____

6. Draw a box around the sentence that tells the main idea.

7. List two details that support the main idea.

   _____

   _____

© Rainbow Bridge Publishing

Assessment Test (continued)

Answer questions 8–11.

8. Leo found the buried treasure because he carefully followed the directions on the map. Write the part of the sentence that is the cause.

_____

Write the part of the sentence that is the effect.

_____

9. If Shelby wears a white coat, carries a stethoscope, and listens to patients' heartbeats throughout the day, what conclusion can you draw about her occupation?

_____

10. Compare and contrast two occupations. Then, use the Venn diagram below to show how these occupations are similar and different. Label the parts of your diagram and give it a title.

Example: Both a clown and a teacher work with children, but a clown wears funny make-up and a costume, and a teacher dresses professionally.

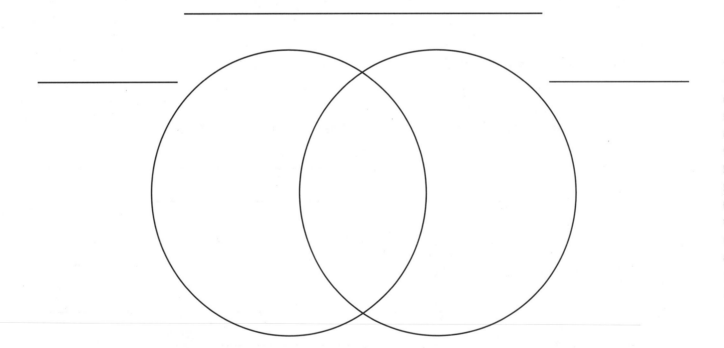

11. On another sheet of paper, draw a treasure map. Write directions, in sequence, to lead explorers to the treasure.

Assessment Test

Read the passage below and answer questions 12–17.

It was dark. The sky was bluish black with pinpoint stars winking in the distance. The leafless trees stretched their shivering arms toward the sky. Meg and Maddie huddled against Mom's legs, pulling the blanket tight against the cold. They were filled with anticipation. The conditions were right; the newscaster had announced that the solar winds were traveling toward Earth. It just had to happen tonight. Orion's Belt rose slowly in the southeastern sky. The Big Dipper hovered, waiting for a scoop of color. A slight shimmer started in the west, a hint of faded blue teasing the eyes. Was it real? Slowly, the color intensified. Greens flowed through the sky like fingers from the north, reaching south and rolling in waves from east to west and back again. Then, the fingers turned red, an awesome color that contrasted vividly with the velvet black sky and the waves of blue and green lights. The aurora borealis, or northern lights, shimmered spectacularly across the sky for 10 minutes, then dimmed, faded, and disappeared. The girls sat speechless, hoping for an encore, but slowly the cold seeped into the awe. Shivering, they gathered their blankets and Mom's chair and walked silently back into the welcoming house.

12. Which of the following events happens third?

    A. The newscaster announced that conditions were right to see the northern lights.

    B. The northern lights shimmered spectacularly across the sky.

    C. Meg and Maddie huddled against their mother's legs.

    D. Meg and Maddie gathered their blankets and their mother's chair and went inside.

13. In which season does the story take place? _____

    How do you know? _____

14. Which of the following best defines the word *encore*?

    A. a repeat performance   **B.** an additional blanket

    C. a shimmering light   **D.** a shooting star

15. What do you think happens next? _____

_____

16. Write the sentence that is a simile. _____

_____

_____

17. Write an antonym for the word *awesome*. _____

Assessment Review

Check Assessment Test answers using the answer key. Match the questions with incorrect answers to the sections. To provide extra practice in problem areas, refer to the pages listed under each section.

1. holds, contains
2. unlikely
3. won, answers will vary
4. A library is a treasure chest.
5. Students should underline the phrase: *A bird in the hand is worth two in the bush.* Answers will vary, but should express the idea that what you have is more valuable than what you do not have.
6. A box should be drawn around the sentence: *Both libraries and treasure chests hold valuable riches.*
7. Answers will vary but may include: the pleasure of reading a good book can last a lifetime and books can transport readers to imaginary worlds.

8. cause—He carefully followed the directions on the map.; effect—Leo found the buried treasure.
9. Shelby is a doctor.
10. Answers will vary.
11. Answers will vary.
12. B.
13. It is winter. It is cold outside and the trees are bare.
14. A.
15. Answers will vary
16. Greens flowed through the sky like fingers from the north, reaching south and rolling in waves from east to west and back again.
17. Answers will vary.

Number(s)	Skill	Activity Page(s)
1 and 17	synonyms and antonyms	9–10
2	prefixes and suffixes	18–19
3	homophones	11
4 and 16	similes and metaphors	20
5	idioms	21
6 and 7	main idea	28–30, 33–34
8	cause and effect	53–54, 69, 78, 80
9	making inferences	60–63, 73, 77
10	compare and contrast	50–51, 72
11	following directions	44–47, 84
12	sequencing	23–27, 30
9 and 13	drawing conclusions	64–67
14	using context clues	15–16, 76
15	predicting outcomes	58–59, 68

Complete the puzzle (page 10) using words from the boxes below. Choose synonyms for **Across** clues and antonyms for **Down** clues.

ACROSS		DOWN	
1. entertain	**15.** disbelief	**1.** detest	**13.** kind
4. arrived	**16.** brim	**2.** above	**15.** reality
6. discontinue	**19.** jimmy	**3.** entrance	**17.** love
7. urge	**21.** cure	**4.** gloom	**18.** odd
8. extra	**23.** permit	**5.** confident	**19.** fancy
9. obtain	**25.** appearance	**6.** unite	**20.** whisper
12. vase	**26.** flow	**10.** maintain	**22.** hint
13. hug	**27.** lengthy	**11.** far	**24.** refreshed
14. path	**29.** each	**12.** lovely	**25.** busy
	30. powerful		**28.** give

Synonyms

drive	pry	edge	earn	every
trail	allow	urn	stop	spare
long	strong	doubt	came	image
amuse	caress	heal	gush	

Antonyms

cruel	exit	near	alter
meek	get	dream	cheer
adore	plain	even	yell
detest	ugly	separate	beg
under	idle	weary	

Complete the puzzle using the clues (page 9).

Which One?

Homophones are words that are pronounced the same but are spelled differently and have different meanings.

Example: There is a <u>frieze</u> that goes across the front of city hall.
Water will <u>freeze</u> when the air temperature drops below 32 degrees Fahrenheit.
The game warden at the wildlife refuge <u>frees</u> injured animals when they are well enough to live in the wild on their own.

Write the homophone that completes each sentence in the blank.

1. The Native Americans taught the pilgrims how to plant ___Maize___ .
   (maize, maze)

2. The ___Presence___ of your company is requested at Beth's party.
   (presence, presents)

3. The nurse had trouble finding my ___vein vane___ when he drew my blood.
   (vein, vane)

4. We took a ___cruise___ ship through the Panama Canal.
   (crews, cruise)

5. Eric won a gold ___medal___ in ice-skating for the third year in a row.
   (medal, metal, meddle)

6. The old ___beech___ tree was struck by lightning.
   (beach, beech)

7. That post is ___stationary___, so all furniture must be placed around it.
   (stationery, stationary)

8. A traditional ___rite___ was held for the bishop when he passed away.
   (right, rite, write)

9. When we make bread, we let it rise and then ___knead___ it.
   (need, knead)

10. They cleared the grocery ___aisle isle___ in order to make room for the canned soup display.
    (aisle, isle)

11. I had never seen anyone play the ___lyre___ until I went to the concert.
    (lyre, liar)

12. Aunt Sara received a letter from Grandpa, who used ___sealing___ wax to close the envelope.
    (sealing, ceiling)

Word Relationships

An **analogy** is a comparison or relationship between two or more things that may otherwise not be alike. To complete an analogy, you must first determine what the relationship between the words is. Then, determine which word could be added to keep the relationship the same. The relationships below use synonyms, antonyms, and homophones to demonstrate analogies.

Examples: Alone is to solo as ocean is to sea. (synonym)
Rear is to front as back is to stomach. (antonym)
Week is to weak as hour is to our. (homophone)

Circle the word that best completes each of the following analogies. Then, write on the line whether each sentence uses a synonym, an antonym, or a homophone as the relationship.

1. Mourn is to _morn_ as knight is to night. _dark_
   day   **dark**   **morn**   **armor**

2. One is to several as _~~some~~ few_ is to many. _____
   some   **single**   **few**   **numerous**

3. _reply_ is to answer as question is to response. _____
   reply   **ask**   **what**   **comeback**

4. Secure is to _safe_ as fence is to barrier. _____
   safe   **shelter**   **protection**   **hide**

5. _asleep_ is to awake as glad is to sad. _____
   free   **hold**   **open**   **asleep**

6. Pedal is to _peddle_ as tense is to tents. _____
   medal   **pump**   **cease**   **peddle**

7. Clean is to immaculate as dirty is to _soiled_. _____
   soiled   **dark**   **pure**   **black**

8. General is to specific as _common_ is to rare. _____
   here   **place**   **common**   **exact**

Amazing Analogies

Complete each analogy with a word from the box.

Example: rose : flower : : oak: ____tree____

1. rind : _____lemon_____ : : skin : apple

2. day : week : : month : ____year____

3. _____aunnt_____ : niece : : uncle : nephew

4. pig : pork : : _____cow_____ : beef

5. push : shove : : pull : ____haul____

6. read : book : : _____write_____ : paper

7. palm : hand : : ____sole____ : foot

8. _____up_____ : down : : ascend : descend

9. collar : _____neck_____ : : cuff : wrist

10. when : time : : where : ____place____

11. celery : ____stalk____ : : lettuce : leaf

12. worm : ____fish____ : : cheese : mouse

13. two : ____four____ : : four : eight

14. flower : pot : : ____vine____ : trellis

15. clear : muddy : : ____transparent____ : cloudy

16. ____hungry____ : food : : thirsty : beverage

17. water : ____pool____ : : ice : rink

18. carpenter : wood : : ____masan____ : stone

19. golf : course : : tennis : ____court____

20. painting : art : : soccer : ____sport____

cow
stalk
vine
hungry
lemon
fish
transparent
sport
mason
write
neck
sole
up
year
four
aunt
pool
haul
court
place

13

Analogies

Choose a word from the box below to complete each analogy. Write the word on the line.

~~accept~~	decrease	~~certain~~
~~thoughtless~~	biology	~~closed~~
~~brave~~	~~ferocious~~	future
typical	~~rescue~~	~~deposit~~

1. Active is to inactive as thoughtful is to _thoughtless_ .

2. Public is to private as open is to _closed_ .

3. Permit is to allow as receive is to _accept_ .

4. Eager is to enthusiastic as courageous is to _brave_ .

5. Terror is to horror as save is to _rescue_ .

6. Guess is to estimate as sure is to _certain_ .

7. Mild is to gentle as fierce is to _ferocious_ .

8. Take is to withdraw as put is to _deposit_ .

9. Geology is to mountains as _biology_ is to animals.

10. Unusual is to usual as rare is to _typical_ .

11. Grow is to increase as shrink is to _decrease_ .

12. Yesterday is to tomorrow as past is to _future_ .

Elephants

You may not recognize a word in a sentence, but there are different ways to decide what it means. One way is to identify its part of speech. Another way is to use the other words in the sentence as **clues** to the word's meaning.

Use context clues to help you determine where the words from the box below fit into the story.

enemies	trunk	usually	shower	replaced	food	tusks	wear
bore	upper	difficult	longer	molars	life	water	

An elephant's trunk is both its nose and hands. Its trunk can find **1.** _food_, pick up food, and put food in the elephant's mouth. The **2.** _trunk_ is also a straw. It sucks up **3.** _water_ to drink or to spray over the elephant for a **4.** _shower_. An elephant's eyes are very small, but its sense of smell is very good.

An elephant's **5.** _tusks_ are long incisor teeth that grow from its **6.** _upper_ jaw. They are used to attack **7.** _enimies_, knock down small trees, and dig and **8.** _shower_ into the ground. An elephant has four **9.** _molars_, one on each side of the upper and lower jaw. Because the elephant's food is **10.** _bore_ to chew, these molars **11.** _wear_ out, but they are **12.** _usally_ by others that grow behind them. This happens five times during an elephant's **13.** _life_. When the last molars wear out, the elephant can no **14.** _loger_ feed itself, and it will die. An elephant **15.** _replaced_ lives for approximately about 65 years.

Check the Meaning

Some words have more than one **meaning**. The context of the sentence can help you determine the correct meaning of the word.

Example: The cowboy wore spurs and **chaps** when he went on a roundup.

Possible definitions: 1. leather leggings connected by a belt and worn over regular pants
                          2. men

(The sentence includes clues to help you determine that the first definition is being used.)

Circle the best definition for the boldfaced word in each sentence below.

1. The feather bed was warm and very **light** to carry.

   set fire to   lamp   not heavy

2. Jenny's father took a picture of her riding **bareback** on her new pony.

   without a saddle   nothing covering the back   went back

3. Woodwind players often keep extra **reeds** handy in case the ones that they are using split.

   tall grasses   arrows   thin pieces of wood or plastic

4. We carried the new **bureau** to the second floor and put it in Tim's room.

   department of government   chest of drawers   administrative unit

5. The teacher asked Susan to **divide** 105 by 15.

   separate into equal parts   a gap between two places   distribute parts

6. The voice teacher had his student sing a **scale** as a warm-up exercise.

   a machine to measure weight   a graduated series of notes   climb

7. David did the **right** thing when he turned in the wallet that he found.

   proper   opposite of left   show ownership

8. Chrissy always **trails** behind looking for wildlife when we go hiking.

   paths   pursues   lags

16

Multiple Meanings

You have learned about homophones like *to*, *too*, and *two*. They are words that are pronounced alike but are spelled differently and may have different meanings. They also may be different parts of speech. Notice the differences in pronunciation, meaning, and part of speech of *permit* in the example below.

Example: He has a *permit* that allows him to go through the gate.

Do not *permit* him to come through the gate.

Use a homograph to complete each sentence pair below.

1. Fred was going to _____ the play he wrote.

   My mother says that the Green Grocer sells the best _____ in town.

2. The _____ blew so hard that the windows in our house rattled.

   _____ up the string on the yo-yo before you begin to play with it.

3. The temperature of the pool's water was _____ .

   The union and company officers had to hire someone to _____ their labor negotiations.

4. Rachel and I went to shop for our father's _____ by ourselves.

   My mom is going to _____ our state governor at next week's Community Lecture Series.

5. The secretary kept a _____ of everything that was discussed at the meeting.

   We had our dad _____ the baseball game on television because we were going out to dinner.

6. My aunt was chosen to _____ the symphony orchestra.

   The boy's _____ during the meeting was not appropriate.

From the Beginning

A **prefix** is a group of letters added to the beginning of a base word to change its meaning.

Example: im + probable = improbable

Read the following prefixes and their meanings. Use them to complete the activities below.

mid = middle	im = not	tele = at a distance
post = after	super = above, outside	sub = below
uni = one, single		

Underline the base words in the words below. Then, write the meanings of the words with their prefixes.

1.   midstream _____

2.   postgraduate _____

3.   improper _____

4.   unicolor _____

5.   subzero _____

Complete the following sentences using words from the box.

subcategory	telescope	immobilize
midterm	superhuman	

6.   There was a man at the circus who performed _____ feats.

7.   I can see the stars at night much better through a _____.

8.   All of the courts are a _____ of the department of justice.

9.   The doctor put a splint on my finger to

_____ it.

10. My brother studied hard for his _____ exam in chemistry.

Base Changes

A **suffix** is a group of letters that is added to the end of a base word to change its meaning.

Example: danger + ous = dangerous

Read the following suffixes and their meanings. Use them to complete the activities below.

ly = like in manner, relating
ance = condition or state of being
al = related to
ship = quality of or having the office of

ous = have qualities of
ish = likeness
ist = one who does, or is skilled at
ant, ent = one who performs

Underline the base words in the words. Then, write the meanings of the words with their suffixes.

1.   <u>contest</u>ant _____

2.   <u>leader</u>ship _____

3.   <u>courage</u>ous _____

4.   <u>sweet</u>ly _____

5.   <u>lobby</u>ist _____

Complete the following paragraph using words from the box.

timely	reddish	abruptly	mechanical	carefully
specialist	easily	resident	generous	patiently

The 6. __resident__ of the 7. __reddish__ apartment building was

a 8. __specialist__ in his field at the hospital. On the way to work, his car stopped

9. __abruptly__ because of 10. __mechanical__

problems. He 11. __patiently__ waited for a tow truck. The serviceman

12. __carefully__ loaded the car onto his truck. The specialist 13. __easily__

found another ride to work from a 14. __generous__ friend. The

specialist's car was fixed in a 15. __timely__ manner.

Comparisons

> **Similes** and **metaphors** are comparisons. Similes often use *like, as,* or *than* to compare two things. Metaphors are implied comparisons. Both compare two unlike things.
>
> **Example of a simile:** The sprinter *ran like a deer* the last 50 feet of the race.
>
> **Example of a metaphor:** His hair *was an uncombed stringy mop.*

Read the sentences below. Write *S* on the line if the comparison is a simile. Write *M* on the line if the comparison is a metaphor.

_____ **1.** Meg babbled on and on like a brook about her baby brother.

_____ **2.** The boys' eyes were as big as saucers when the magician pulled a mouse out of Larry's shirt.

_____ **3.** Some news travels like the wind.

_____ **4.** This piece of candy is as hard as a rock.

_____ **5.** The moon was a lantern that lit up the night sky.

_____ **6.** The dark storm clouds were dragons spitting fire.

_____ **7.** Joe is a dirty rat to squeal about the surprise!

_____ **8.** The fog is as thick as pea soup.

_____ **9.** The soldier stood as straight as an arrow.

_____ **10.** The puppy ran around like a tornado.

_____ **11.** The sky was a red ceiling during the fireworks display.

_____ **12.** After the blizzard, the highway was as smooth as glass.

_____ **13.** The flower bed is a rainbow on the ground.

_____ **14.** The lawyer was a tiger concerning his client's innocence.

_____ **15.** The soprano in the opera sings like a canary.

Summer Bridge Reading RB-904095

What Does It Mean?

> An **idiom** is a figure of speech that says one thing and means another. It is often a phrase.
>
> **Example:** It was quiet before Sam **broke the ice** by telling a funny story. (Did Sam really break the ice? No, he told a story to make people feel more comfortable.)

Write the letter of the definition that best describes the meaning of each bold idiom.

A. a different subject

B. out of place

C. had the same problem

D. lost the opportunity

E. to talk a lot

F. did it right

G. to cause trouble

H. try it out

_____ 1. The doctor was **a fish out of water** when she attended a meeting for hospital accountants.

_____ 2. My cousins stayed up late **to shoot the breeze** at our family reunion.

_____ 3. The factory worker did not want **to make waves** for fear that he might lose his job.

_____ 4. The school's finance committee was discussing what playground equipment it would buy when Mrs. Jones raised a question about buying books for the library. The chairperson of the committee said, "That's **a horse of another color**."

_____ 5. You should **test the waters** before making a major decision.

_____ 6. The food committee **hit the nail on the head** when it planned the menu for the school picnic.

_____ 7. Everyone on the highway **was in the same boat** when the truck carrying eggs overturned during rush hour.

_____ 8. My father was angry at himself because he **missed the boat** when he did not buy property on the lake.

21

What a Character!

Personification is when an inanimate object, plant, or animal is described as having human qualities. It might have human characteristics or act or talk like a person.

Example: The daisies' faces smiled when they received a drink of water. (The daisies have the human qualities of having faces and smiling.)

Underline what is being personified in each sentence. Then, write the word or words that identify the personification. **Example:** The <u>trees</u> moaned unhappily as the wind bent their branches. (moaned unhappily)

1.   The first-place trophy stood proudly on the shelf in Charlie's room.

   _____

2.   Since we could not go out to play, we watched from our window as the clouds spit diamonds toward the ground.

   _____

3.   Autumn leaves seemed to sing as they danced across the lawn.

   _____

4.   Horns honked angrily as drivers became more impatient.

   _____

5.   The sun played hide-and-seek with me as it popped in and out of the clouds.

   _____

6.   The clouds marched across the sky ahead of the storm.

   _____

7.   The house eagerly waited for the new owners to arrive.

   _____

Summer Bridge Reading RB-904095

The Anasazi

Putting a series of events in order is called **sequencing**.

Read the passage.

One prehistoric civilization of the southwestern United States was the Anasazi. We do not know what the Anasazi called themselves. *Anasazi* is the name given to them by archaeologists and scholars who have studied prehistoric Native Americans of the Southwest. *Anasazi* is a Navajo word that means "ancient enemy." Over time, the word has come to mean "ancient people." Some modern tribes prefer the term *Ancestral Puebloans* to the term *Anasazi*. However, *Anasazi* is the term that is most commonly used to describe the early people of the southwestern United States.

The Anasazi most likely came to the Southwest around 100 B.C. They built simple homes with sticks and mud in shallow caves along canyon walls. They relied heavily on foods that they grew themselves, such as corn and squash. They were expert basket weavers, and therefore, the first Anasazi phase is named the Early Basket Maker Period. This period lasted until around 500 A.D.

The next Anasazi phase is the Modified Basket Maker Period. These Anasazi wanted to be closer to their crops, so they built their homes in open areas near the land they farmed. Their homes were called *pit houses* because they were built partially underground. During this period, the Anasazi still made baskets, but they also began making clay pots. Beans became an important crop because beans could now be cooked over a fire in a clay pot. During this time, the Anasazi began wearing turquoise jewelry and using a bow and arrow for hunting.

The Anasazi's third phase, the Developmental Pueblo Period, began around 700 A.D. Their homes were now aboveground, but they built kivas, or ceremonial rooms, partially underground. They made pottery for two purposes: cooking and beauty.

The Great Pueblo Period began around 1050 A.D. During this period, the Anasazi built cliff dwellings that looked like some of today's apartment buildings. They used ladders to get into the upper stories. They could pull these ladders inside to keep enemies from entering. Sometimes,

several of these cliff dwellings were built near each other to form communities. These communities sometimes became the center for an entire region. Trade with nearby tribes began during this period.

It is not entirely clear what became of the Anasazi. Some people believe that the Anasazi were victims of a drought that caused them to abandon their pueblos and communities. Other people believe that fights with other tribes were responsible for the Anasazi's disappearance. By 1540 A.D., only three of the Anasazi's major pueblo clusters remained occupied.

23

The Anasazi

Number the following events below to show the correct sequence of the passage (page 23).

_____ **A.** The third phase began around 700 A.D., and it is named the Developmental Pueblo Period.

_____ **B.** This first phase is the Early Basket Maker Period.

_____ **C.** What actually happened to the Anasazi remains a mystery.

_____ **D.** The Anasazi probably came to the southwestern United States around 100 B.C.

_____ **E.** The Great Pueblo Period began around 1050 A.D.

_____ **F.** The second phase began after 500 A.D., and it is named the Modified Basket Maker Period.

_____ **G.** When several of the cliff dwellings were built near each other, they formed a larger community.

_____ **H.** They grew corn and squash and were excellent basket makers.

_____ **I.** The homes of the last phase were similar to some of today's apartment buildings.

_____ **J.** During the Developmental Pueblo Period, the Anasazi's homes were aboveground while ceremonial rooms, called kivas, were partly underground.

Summer Bridge Reading RB-904095

Freddie's New Home

The following groups of sentences are out of order. Number each group to show the correct sequence.

A. _____ He did not know anyone in the neighborhood.

_____ He did not live far from the park. Freddie thought that if he walked there, he might meet some new friends.

_____ Freddie had just moved into his new home on Elm Street.

B. _____ When he got to the park, Freddie saw some boys playing baseball.

_____ The boys reluctantly agreed to let him play.

_____ He introduced himself and asked if he could play with them.

C. _____ His team ended up winning.

_____ Later, when his team was batting, Freddie scored four runs.

_____ When Freddie's team was in the field, he made a couple of spectacular outs.

_____ After that, the boys were always ringing his doorbell and asking him to come to the park to play baseball.

D. _____ They found out that they shared some of these interests.

_____ For the rest of the summer, Freddie enjoyed playing with the boys.

_____ At the end of the summer, all of the boys were good friends—on and off the baseball field.

_____ Once, Freddie invited the boys to his house so that they could learn more about his other interests.

Space Exploration

A **time line** shows dates and events in the order they happened.

The time line below shows important events in the history of space exploration. Study the time line, and answer the questions (page 27).

Oct. 4, 1957 The Union of Soviet Socialist Republics (USSR) launched *Sputnik 1*, the first man-made satellite.

Nov. 3, 1957 The USSR launched *Sputnik 2*, which carried the first space traveler, a dog.

Apr. 12, 1961 The USSR launched *Vostok 1*, the first manned flight, with Yuri Gagarin.

Feb. 20, 1962 John Glenn, aboard *Mercury 6*, was the first American to orbit Earth.

Oct. 16–19, 1963 The USSR's Valentina Tereshkova, who was aboard *Vostok 6*, was the first woman in space.

Mar. 18, 1965 The USSR completed the first space walk from *Voskhod 2*.

Dec. 21–27, 1968 *Apollo 8* from the United States (U.S.) was the first manned flight to orbit the moon.

July 16–24, 1969 U.S. astronauts Neil Armstrong and Edwin Aldrin, aboard the United States' *Apollo 11*, made the first moon landing.

May 14, 1973 The first U.S. space station was established.

Dec. 4, 1978 The *Pioneer Venus* from the United States entered the orbit of Venus.

Apr. 12–14, 1981 The United States flew the space shuttle *Columbia*, a reusable spacecraft.

Use the time line (page 26) to order each set of events below.

1.   Number the following space missions in the order that they occurred.

_____   *Vostok 6*

_____   *Sputnik 2*

_____   space shuttle *Columbia*

_____   *Apollo 8*

2.   Write the letter of the space explorer in front of the date of the mission.

_____   July 16–24, 1969   **A.**   Yuri Gagarin

_____   February 20, 1962   **B.**   Neil Armstrong

_____   April 12, 1961   **C.**   Valentina Tereshkova

_____   October 16–19, 1963   **D.**   John Glenn

3.   Number the following events in the order that they occurred.

_____   the first U.S. space station

_____   the first man-made satellite

_____   the first woman in space

_____   the first manned flight to orbit the moon

_____   the first space walk

_____   the first moon landing

Extra! Make a time line of important events that happened at your school or home.

You Have the Idea!

> The **main idea** identifies the main point (or points) in a story. The main idea in a paragraph is often stated in the first or second sentence and summed up in the final sentence.

Circle the letter next to the main idea of each paragraph.

1. The ancient Egyptians used a reed, called papyrus, to make paper. They cut the stem into thin slices. They laid some slices lengthwise and placed others across them. Next, they moistened the layers of papyrus slices with water, put a heavy weight on the layers to press them together, and dried them. When the layers were dry, they stuck together in a sheet. The Egyptians rubbed the dried sheet until it was smooth enough to write on. Sometimes, sheets were joined together to make long scrolls.

   A. how papyrus was made   **B.** how paper was made

   C. definition of papyrus   **D.** ancient Egypt

2. In ancient times, only a few people knew how to write. Most people who needed something written down asked scribes to write for them. A scribe was someone who could write.

   A. ancient times   **B.** ancient alphabets

   C. scribes   **D.** people in ancient times

3. A pyramid is a large structure with a square base and four triangular sides that come to a point at the top. The ancient Egyptians built pyramids as tombs in which the bodies of their kings and queens were placed. Before the bodies were placed in the pyramids, they were mummified. The mummies were placed in the tombs along with personal belongings and household items. The Egyptians hoped to hide and preserve the bodies, because they believed that as long as their bodies were preserved their souls would live forever. The remains of several pyramids can still be seen in Egypt, but the tombs are empty. Grave robbers looted the graves.

   A. burying the dead in ancient Egypt   **B.** how pyramids were built

   C. use of pyramids in ancient Egypt   **D.** remains of the pyramids

Writing a Main Idea

All of the ideas in a paragraph are clues that help you understand the main idea.

Read each group of words. Decide how the words could be related if they were found in a paragraph together. Then, write a paragraph using the words. Be sure to include a sentence telling the main idea. Circle that sentence.

1. five candles   chocolate cake   Peter's day   a lot of presents

   _____

   _____

   _____

   _____

   _____

2. amusement park   roller coaster   cotton candy   bumper cars

   _____

   _____

   _____

   _____

   _____

3. science fair   blue ribbon   judges   project

   _____

   _____

   _____

   _____

   _____

Caring for the Environment

Below are groups of three sentences in a mixed-up order. One sentence in each group is the main idea. One sentence supports the main idea, and one concludes the idea expressed by the other two sentences. Write *1* on the line following the main idea. Write *2* on the line following the supporting sentence. Write *3* on the line following the concluding sentence.

A.   It is often used to describe where people or animals live. _____

The word *environment* means the surroundings in which a living thing exists. _____

Our environment is made up of the soil, rock, water, vegetation, and air that surround us. _____

B.   Therefore, people should not only learn to protect where they live, but they should also become informed about other environments. _____

Varied world environments, such as wetlands, tropical rain forests, and grasslands, need protection. _____

If any part of the earth is harmed, all living things are affected. _____

C.   Grasslands cover much of North America's midwest. _____

The region plays an important agricultural role in the United States. _____

These lands are used mostly for grazing animals and growing crops. _____

D.   Sometimes, people want to drain these areas so that they can be developed. _____

But the wetlands of the world should be protected because they contain rare animals and plants. _____

Some environments, such as swamps and marshes, are wet. _____

E.   Now, many organizations work to protect the tropical rain forests. _____

Large areas of forest land in tropical rain forests are being cut to make room for roads, towns, factories, and ranches. _____

Many people realize how important the rain forests are to the health of the planet, and they want to save the forests before they are destroyed forever. _____

Summer Bridge Reading RB-904095

Shiloh

An author includes many **details** to help readers better understand a story. Details provide a clearer picture of all of the story elements, such as characters, setting, and plot.

Read the summary of Phyllis Reynolds Naylor's book _Shiloh_ (Aladdin, 2000). Use details from the summary to complete the puzzle. The bold spaces will tell you what award this book received.

In _Shiloh_, an award-winning book, 11-year-old Marty Preston tells about what happens when a dog follows him home. Marty lives with his parents and two sisters, Becky and Dara Lynn, in the hills above Friendly. Friendly is a small town in West Virginia near Sisterville. On a Sunday afternoon after a big dinner of rabbit and sweet potatoes, Marty goes for a walk along the river. During his walk, Marty spies a short-haired dog. The dog, a beagle with black and brown spots, does not make a sound as he watches and follows Marty. From the dog's behavior, Marty suspects that the dog has been mistreated. Since he found the dog near the old Shiloh schoolhouse, Marty calls the dog Shiloh. Marty soon discovers that Shiloh belongs to mean Judd Travers. After returning Shiloh to Judd, Marty contemplates how he can earn enough money to buy the dog from him. Before Marty can solve this problem, he is faced with a difficult decision.

1. In what town does Marty live?
2. How old is Marty?
3. What kind of potatoes did the family eat on Sunday?
4. What kind of meat did they eat?
5. What kind of dog is Shiloh?
6. Write the last name of Shiloh's owner.
7. Name one of Marty's sisters.
8. What adjective was used to describe Judd Travers?
9. What is Marty's last name?
10. What day does Marty find Shiloh?
11. Who tells the story in the book?
12. Marty finds the dog near what schoolhouse?

31

Wonton Soup

Read the story below and answer the following questions.

Lin Yu-Hua was 10 years old when her family moved to the United States from China. She was excited about coming to the United States but a little nervous, too. In China, she always ate her grandmother's homemade wonton soup. Lin enjoyed helping her grandmother make the soup, and she would miss that.

In the United States, Lin met a girl named Jennifer in her class. Lin liked going to Jennifer's house to eat pizza and watch movies. Sometimes, Lin spent the night with Jennifer, too. Lin's family did not have a TV or a DVD player yet. Her father and mother were trying to get the necessities in the house first. Lin had just gotten her new bed. Later, they would get a television.

One day, Lin invited Jennifer over while her mother was making several Chinese foods for dinner. One of the things her mother made was the delicious wonton soup that her grandmother often made. Mrs. Yu-Hua was working on the noodles for the soup while Jennifer and Lin measured the water and cut up the onions for the broth. Soon, each of them had their parts finished, and the soup was placed on the stove to cook. Then, Mr. Yu-Hua came in and complimented the cooks on the wonderful smell.

When the soup was ready, the girls prepared the table. Lin brought chopsticks. Jennifer was surprised that she was going to have to eat with chopsticks! Mrs. Yu-Hua placed the rice, pork, and a platter of mixed Chinese vegetables on the table. Lin served the soup in bowls. The family sat down with their guest and began eating. Jennifer discovered that she was good at using the chopsticks, and the soup was excellent. The Yu-Hua family was very happy to share their stories of China and their trip west that evening at dinner. Lin decided that her grandmother would be proud of the soup, and she would be pleased to know that her granddaughter had made a friend.

---

1. What country is Lin from?

_____

2. What food do the girls eat at Jennifer's house?

_____

3. How many different foods does Lin's mother make the night Jennifer visits for dinner?

_____

4. Jennifer discovers she is very good at using _____ .

Sod Houses

Read the passage.

In the 19th century, many American pioneers moved west to start new lives. Many pioneers settled the Great Plains, a region of the midwestern United States. When they found the land where they wanted to settle, they had many important tasks to complete. They had to plant gardens and crops. They had to dig wells. They may have needed to prepare for winter. Since there were so many things to do when they first settled, they often built temporary houses. These homes had to be strong enough to protect the settlers but not take too long to build. A few years later, when their lives were more established and they had money to buy materials, the pioneers built more permanent homes.

One kind of temporary home was a sod house. Sod houses were built where trees were scarce, and they were made of packed dirt. The pioneers cut the dirt into brick shapes from the ground with plows and axes. As they plowed their fields, the pioneers skimmed off the top layer of tough sod to use for the sod bricks. At the same time, they freed the looser soil below for planting. The sod bricks were thick with roots. The pioneers stacked them together much like regular bricks to form a house. As the sod house settled, it became stronger. The roots helped cement the bricks together as they grew from one brick to another.

A well-made sod house was comfortable and dry. The windows and doors were often made with wooden frames and real glass. A roof could be made with straw and dirt, or a wooden roof could be covered with more sod. The sod house stayed cool in the summer and warm in the winter. But, a poorly made sod house leaked when it rained and allowed wind to seep through the cracks.

The pioneers who lived in sod houses often had company in their homes. Snakes, insects, and other small critters were very comfortable in the sod bricks. It was not uncommon to see a snake making itself at home on a window sill or a mouse scurrying around on the floor. Other creatures and bits of dirt often dropped from the ceiling, as well.

The pioneers made use of natural resources to survive. Sod houses are just one symbol of their determination to survive the harsh frontier life of the American Midwest.

33

Fill in the outline below to take notes on the article "Sod Houses" (page 33).

First Paragraph

main idea: _____

details: _____

_____

Second Paragraph

main idea: _____

details: _____

_____

Third Paragraph

main idea: _____

details: _____

_____

Fourth Paragraph

main idea: _____

details: _____

_____

Fifth Paragraph

main idea: _____

details: _____

_____

Ty Cobb

Read the passage below.

Many people argue about whether Ty Cobb was the greatest baseball player of all time. However, almost everyone agrees that he was the meanest player of all time.

Ty Cobb played most of his 24-year professional career for the Detroit Tigers at the beginning of the 1900s. He was the game's fiercest competitor both on and off the field. His temper and attitude provoked injuries and fights with opponents and sometimes even with his own teammates. According to legend, Cobb sharpened the spikes on his cleats before every game to intimidate and even injure other players. He acted as though he owned the base paths, and he often proclaimed that no opposing player was going to get in his way.

Cobb had good reason to believe that he did own the base paths. His stolen-base record of 96 in 1915 stood for 47 years. His batting accomplishments are also legendary. He had a lifetime batting average of 0.367. He hit 297 triples. He boasted 4,191 hits. Cobb played 23 straight seasons in which he hit over 0.300. During three of those seasons, he hit over 0.400, topped by a 0.420 mark in 1911. His statistics include 1,937 runs batted in (RBIs) and 2,245 runs scored. Cobb led the league five times in stolen bases, and for nine consecutive years—and 12 times overall—Cobb's batting average was the best in the league. He stole 892 bases in his 24 years at bat.

Because he was from Georgia, Ty Cobb was also known as "The Georgia Peach." He was the first player elected into the Baseball Hall of Fame. He even beat the legendary and popular Babe Ruth. When he retired, he held virtually every hitting record that was kept. Although people still love to hate Ty Cobb, he is a baseball player to remember.

Answer the questions in complete sentences.

1. What did Ty Cobb do that was mean?

_____

2. Why was Cobb elected to the Baseball Hall of Fame?

_____

3. What does it mean that Cobb "owned" the base paths?

_____

4. What was Ty Cobb's nickname?

_____

It can be difficult to read statistics in a paragraph. Draw a bar graph in the space below, and use it to plot some of Ty Cobb's statistics. Add as many columns as needed. Label the chart and fill in the relevant details.

Read the questions on the left and the answers on the right. Draw a line from each question to its answer.

Questions	Answers
What would you like to have for dinner tonight?	My favorite is Spaghetti. I love their music.
Have you counted the number of trees on the property?	Yes, Potter came in first place.
Have you read any of the *Harry Potter* books?	Lasagna would be my first choice.
What is your favorite rock band?	I read that there are 898. The monument is surrounded by 50 U.S. flags.
How many steps are there on the way to the top of the Washington Monument?	Yes, I read the first and second ones. They were both exciting.
Did you see Potter running in the race around the lake?	Yes, there are 14 maples, 10 oaks, and 2 others that I don't recognize.

Frosty

> The most important **characters** in a story are called main characters. They seem to be brought to life by their actions. Details from the story help the reader better understand the personalities of the characters.

Read the story below and answer the following questions.

Emily saw a gray, long-haired cat on her way to the park. She stopped to pet it and find out if it had a collar with an identification tag. It did not. Emily walked on to meet her friends, and the cat followed her. Emily and her friends played on the swings and other playground equipment. The cat followed the girls from one place to another and watched them play. When it was time to go, Emily waved good-bye to her friends and walked home. As she walked, she noticed that the cat was following her home.

When Emily got to her house, she went in the kitchen door. The cat sat outside the closed screen door and watched Emily eat her lunch. Emily knew that it was not a good idea to feed a stray pet, but the cat seemed very hungry. Emily put some turkey on a plate and gave it to the cat.

After lunch, Emily decided to clean the cat. She began to brush the cat, and its fur became lighter as Emily removed dirt from the cat's long hair. It seemed that the gray cat was really a white cat!

When she finished brushing the cat, Emily drew some sketches of it. With a poster pen, she wrote its description, where she found it, and a phone number that the owner could call. That afternoon, Emily put her notices up in the neighborhood. She also called the animal shelter to report the found cat.

There were no responses after a few days, and the cat had become her friend. Emily asked her parents if she could keep the cat, and they agreed that it was a nice pet. Emily decided to call it Frosty because it was now as white as snow.

1. Who is the main character in this story? _____

2. Circle the two words that describe this character.

   frustrated   **careless**   **caring**   **tough**   **resourceful**

3. List three ways that the character demonstrates the character traits that you circled above.

   _____

   _____

Becoming Good Neighbors

Read the story and answer the following questions.

Billy and Roger were next-door neighbors and were in the same class at Central School. Billy was probably the brightest student in the class. Roger was definitely the strongest and the best athlete in the school. The boys often rode to school together in the morning with one of their parents, but in the afternoon, they came home separately. Roger usually stayed and played either soccer or basketball with some of the older boys. Sometimes, Billy watched, but usually he went home and did his homework or read a book.

One day, Billy asked if he could join Roger's after-school soccer game. Roger answered, "No, you are too small and not strong enough." All of the other boys laughed as they headed out to the field. Billy was crushed. He went home and studied for the next day's science test.

When Billy and Roger got to the classroom the next day, their teacher said that she would give the test right away. That way, they could get their scores back at the end of the day. Everything on the test was material Billy had studied, so he had no trouble answering the questions. Billy noticed that Roger had barely written anything. When the tests were returned, Billy had "100%" written at the top of his paper, and on Roger's test, there was a note saying that he must take the test again. Billy offered to help Roger study for the test.

The next morning on their way to school, Roger invited Billy to play with his friends after school. He encouraged Billy by telling him that he would teach him how to play the games.

1. Who are the main characters in the story? _____

2. Circle two characteristics that Billy demonstrates in the story.

   helpful   **athletic**   **selfish**   **studious**

3. Circle two characteristics that Roger demonstrates in the story before the science test.

   athletic   **unfriendly**   **studious**   **caring**

4. Circle two characteristics that Roger demonstrates after the science test.

   frustrated   **considerate**   **appreciative**   **threatening**

The Supreme Court

Read the passage.

Originally, the number of justices who sat on the U.S. Supreme Court varied from six to 10. From 1869 to this day, the Court has had nine justices: one chief justice and eight associate justices.

The Court may consider 5,000 cases each year, but usually, only several hundred cases come before it. The cases are either of national importance or challenge a law based on constitutional grounds.

Every case that comes before the Court is given the name of the parties involved. If Mr. Jones is suing the U.S. government, the case is called *Jones v. the United States*. When the justices decide a case, it becomes a precedent, which means that the decision becomes the basis for future rulings.

All Supreme Court justices are appointed by the president and approved by the Senate. Supreme Court justices may hold their seats until they die. However, if a justice acts improperly or shows corruptness, the justice may be impeached and removed from the Court.

The Court's most important duty is to maintain the laws as laid out in the U.S. Constitution. The authors of the Constitution could not have known what life would be like in the 21st century. Therefore, it is up to the Court to interpret the Constitution as it relates to current practices.

Summer Bridge Reading RB-904095

The Supreme Court

Circle the facts that complete the sentences below.

1. Justices may be _____ from the Court if they act improperly.

   accused and barred   blamed and banned

   fired   impeached and removed

2. Currently, the Court has _____ justices.

   more   one chief justice and eight associate

   fewer   one chief justice and nine associate

3. The Supreme Court hears _____ cases each year.

   5,000   several hundred

   100   about 100

4. The Court must _____ the U.S. Constitution in light of today's times.

   adjust   interpret

   reverse   rewrite

5. The cases that come before the Court are either _____ or they challenge laws based on constitutional grounds.

   constitutional law   of national importance

   not important   state laws

6. The Court's most important function is to _____ as defined in the U.S. Constitution.

   keep law and order   appoint federal court judges

   maintain the laws   update the laws

7. Every case that comes before the Court is given the name of the _____.

   U.S. government   deciding justice

   person suing   parties involved

8. Supreme Court justices are named by the president and _____ by the Senate.

   appointed   announced

   approved   applauded

Chart Facts

Facts about a certain subject are often listed in a **chart**. A chart makes it easier to compare the facts. Be sure to read all of the information carefully.

Twenty-nine percent of Earth is land. This land is divided into seven continents. Use the following chart to record information about the continents (page 43).

	Area (in square miles)	Highest Mountain (in feet)	Lowest Point (in feet below sea level)	Longest River (in miles)
Africa	11,608,000 (30,065,000 sq. km)	Kilimanjaro 19,340 (5,895 m)	Lake Assal 512 (156 m)	Nile 4,160 (6,690 km)
Antarctica	5,100,000 (13,209,000 sq. km)	Vinson Massif 16,864 (5,140 m)	Bentley Subglacial Trench 8,327 (2,538 m)	no rivers
Asia	17,212,000 (44,579,000 sq. km)	Everest 29,035 (8,850 m)	Dead Sea 1,348 (411 m)	Chang (Yangtze) 3,964 (6,380 km)
Australia	3,132,000 (8,112,000 sq. km)	Kosciusko 7,310 (2,228 m)	Lake Eyre 52 (16 m)	Murray-Darling 2,310 (3,720 km)
Europe	3,837,000 (9,938,000 sq. km)	Elbrus 18,510 (5,642 m)	Caspian Sea 92 (28 m)	Volga 2,290 (3,690 km)
North America	9,449,000 (24,474,000 sq. km)	McKinley 20,320 (6,194 m)	Death Valley 282 (86 m)	Missouri 2,540 (4,090 km)
South America	6,879,000 (17,819,000 sq. km)	Aconcagua 22,834 (6,960 m)	Valdes Peninsula 131 (40 m)	Amazon 4,000 (6,440 km)

Answer the following questions using the chart (page 42).

1. List the continents according to size from largest to smallest.

   A. _____

   B. _____

   C. _____

   D. _____

   E. _____

   F. _____

   G. _____

2. How many meters below sea level is Earth's lowest point?_____

3. Which are the two longest rivers? _____

4. Which two continents are about the same size? _____

5. Which continent has the highest point? _____

   Which continent has the longest river?_____

6. List the mountains that are greater than 20,000 feet high.

   _____

7. List the rivers from shortest to longest.

   A. _____

   B. _____

   C. _____

   D. _____

   E. _____

   F. _____

Extra! Write two questions using the chart and answer them.

Summer Bridge Reading RB-904095

In the Right Direction

> Often, **directions** are sequenced steps that help you do something or get somewhere. The steps in directions should be read one at a time and followed exactly.

Most likely, there are several appliances in your home that you use frequently, but rarely consider the steps you take to make them work. Imagine that you have rented your home to someone who has never seen these appliances. Now, you need to leave instructions for how to work some of them. Number the following instructions in a logical order.

A. How to Use the Toaster

_____ Press down the toaster's lever.

_____ Determine how brown you would like your bread. For lightly toasted bread, turn the dial toward 1. For dark toasted bread, turn the dial toward 10.

_____ Place bread, bagel, or English muffin slices in the toaster slots.

B. How to Use the Washing Machine

_____ Next, determine the size of your load. Turn the knob to small, medium, or large.

_____ Gently lay the dirty laundry around the center agitator.

_____ Depending on the size of your wash load, pour between a quarter to a half cup of liquid detergent on the load.

_____ Set the type of wash (regular, permanent press, or delicate), close the lid, and pull out the knob to start the machine.

C. How to Use the DVD Player

_____ Using the up and down arrow buttons on the remote control, select the PLAY MOVIE option.

_____ To remove the DVD, press EJECT.

_____ To turn on the DVD player, press the red button in the top right corner of the remote control.

_____ To open the DVD player, press EJECT. Insert the DVD and then close the DVD player. Using the remote control, press MENU.

_____ When you are finished watching the DVD, press STOP.

© Rainbow Bridge Publishing

44

Summer Bridge Reading RB-904095

Figuring It Out

Complete each set of directions in the spaces.

 A.

1. Draw two vertical, parallel lines.

2. Draw two horizontal, parallel lines that intersect the vertical lines.

3. Draw a circle that intersects every line.

4. Draw an X in the center box.

 B.

1. Write the name of a type of building that rhymes with mouse.

2. Change the middle letter to *N*.

3. Switch the order of the last two letters.

4. Add the 20th letter of the alphabet to the end of the word.

5. What is the word?

 C.

1. Draw a hexagon.

2. Inside of the hexagon, write how many sides it has.

3. Draw three different-sized triangles below it.

4. Shade in the middle triangle.

 D.

1. Write the word that means "words with the same or nearly the same meaning."

2. Beginning with the first *s*, cross out every other letter.

3. Add the second remaining letter between the last two letters.

4. Add a hyphen between the second and third letters.

5. What is the word?

Summer Bridge Reading RB-904095

That's Nonsense!

> **Limericks** are short poems with a specific rhyme pattern and rhythm. They are usually silly or funny. Limericks are five lines long.

The following two limericks were written by Edward Lear. Lear was a famous author known for his nonsense poems and limericks.

> There was an old man of Blackheath,
>
> Whose head was adorned with a wreath,
>
> Of lobsters and spice,
>
> Pickled onions and mice,
>
> That uncommon old man of Blackheath.

> There was an Old Man with a beard,
>
> Who said, "It is just as I feared!—
>
> Two Owls and a Hen,
>
> Four Larks and a Wren,
>
> Have all built their nests in my beard!"

The first, second, and last lines of a limerick end with the same rhyme. The third and fourth lines are shorter and rhyme with each other. The first and last lines are often similar.

When you try to write a limerick, follow these steps:

Step 1: Think of an unusual character to introduce and the name of a place to end the first line.

Step 2: Think of a word that rhymes with the place to end the second line.

Step 3: For the third and fourth lines, think of a problem—a silly thing the character did or the silly way that he looks.

Step 4: Think of what happens to the character because of the problem.

Step 5: For the last line, think of a way to repeat the first line with a variation resulting from the problem.

Example:

Character: silly bird

Place: Peru

Rhyme with Peru: shoe

Problem: bird lived in a shoe

Result: bird was flattened by a foot

> There was a silly bird from Peru,
>
> Who thought the best home was a shoe.
>
> He was as snug as a pin,
>
> When a foot crowded in.
>
> That poor, flat bird from Peru.

Write a limerick. Start by planning your limerick below.

Unusual character: _____

Name of a place: _____

Rhyme with the place: _____

Problem: _____

Result: _____

Use the information you listed above to write the limerick on the lines below. Then, draw a picture of the character in your limerick in the space provided.

Line 1: _____
(Rhyme A)

Line 2: _____
(Rhyme A)

Line 3: _____
(Rhyme B)

Line 4: _____
(Rhyme B)

Line 5: _____
(Rhyme A)

Common Ground

Read each group of words. Circle the letter next to the word or phrase that tells what the words have in common.

1. joyful, miserable, anxious
   A. happiness
   B. sadness
   C. emotions

2. discord, argument, disagreement
   A. conflict
   B. harmony
   C. nation

3. North Sea, Pacific Ocean, Bay of Biscay
   A. bodies of water
   B. continents
   C. U.S. presidents

4. beagle, collie, poodle
   A. dogs
   B. cats
   C. horses

5. hamsters, cats, dogs
   A. amphibians
   B. reptiles
   C. pets

6. car, truck, sedan
   A. dogs
   B. vehicles
   C. structures

7. Abe, Danny, Jenny
   A. dogs
   B. names
   C. places

8. tail, paw, fur
   A. parts of a dog
   B. parts of a person
   C. parts of a car

9. muzzle, snout, beak
   A. noses
   B. ears
   C. eyes

10. apples, grapes, raspberries
    A. nonperishable foods
    B. types of fruit
    C. fruits that grow on trees

Summer Bridge Reading RB-904095

It's Not Like the Rest

Fill in the circle next to the item that does not belong.

1. ○ horse   ○ dog   ○ coffee   ○ ferret

2. ○ car   ○ truck   ○ convertible   ○ pyramid

3. ○ Asia   ○ Australia   ○ Antarctica   ○ Atlantic Ocean

4. ○ street   ○ block   ○ astronomy   ○ neighborhood

5. ○ sea horses   ○ sharks   ○ cats   ○ tropical fish

6. ○ huskies   ○ Siamese cats   ○ collies   ○ beagles

7. ○ tigers   ○ whales   ○ bears   ○ lions

8. ○ leash   ○ gutter   ○ rope   ○ chain

9. ○ happy   ○ disappointed   ○ glad   ○ delighted

10. ○ delighted   ○ miserable   ○ neighbor   ○ anxious

11. ○ yard   ○ yawn   ○ stretch   ○ sleep

12. ○ yam   ○ yellow   ○ certain   ○ yell

13. ○ walked   ○ hurried   ○ worried   ○ green

14. ○ tail   ○ paw   ○ muzzle   ○ jeans

15. ○ button   ○ nose   ○ zipper   ○ pocket

Extra! Answer the following riddle if you can: I am hard. You can build things out of me. If you break me down into tiny pieces, I become sand. I rhyme with what visitors do before you open your door.

What am I? _____

Ships of the Desert

> To **compare** means to note the similarities and differences of subjects. To **contrast** means to show the differences of subjects. By comparing and contrasting, you will better understand the material you read.

Camels were once wild animals in Arabia and Asia, but long ago, they were domesticated. There are two kinds of camels: the one-humped Arabian camel and the two-humped Bactrian camel. Both are useful for doing work, but the Bactrian camel is sturdier, can carry heavier loads, and can withstand cooler climates. Arabian camels, which can be trained for racing, have shorter hair than Bactrian camels. Camels are called "ships of the desert" because they sway when they walk and they are a major means of transportation in the desert.

A camel's hump is actually made up of stored fat that the camel's body uses for food when plant food is not available on long desert walks. Water is not stored in a camel's hump. Water is stored in body tissues and in pouches inside a camel's stomach.

Nomadic people in North Africa and Asia still use camels. Camels carry loads where there are no roads. Also, their hair, hides, meat, and milk are used for clothing and food.

List the similarities and differences of Arabian and Bactrian camels in the chart using the following facts.

- one hump
- shorter hair
- trained for racing
- sway when walk
- used for food and clothing
- sturdier
- hump stores fat for food
- can withstand cooler climates
- two humps

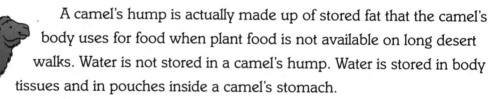

Arabian Camel	Bactrian Camel	Both
_____	_____	_____
_____	_____	_____
_____	_____	_____
_____	_____	_____

Summer Bridge Reading RB-904095

Winter Is a White Owl

Read the poem.

The owl's eyes shine darkly

As the quiet moon at midnight.

So chillingly cold,

So dark and black.

The snow falls gently,

Like the downy feathers

Of the night watcher.

He floats from tree to limb,

Ever watchful,

In the frosty winter night.

The moon casts her pale light

On the soft snow.

Nature is in silent slumber,

Deeply buried

Under a blanket of white crystals.

The owl is alone,

Except for the moon.

All is still.

Extra! To what would you compare winter? Why?

_____

_____

Answer the questions.

1. What images do you see in your mind as you read this poem?

    _____

2. Describe the setting of this poem.

    _____

3. How does the snow fall?

    _____

4. What is the mood of this poem?

    _____

5. Have you ever been in a forest during winter? If so, describe what the experience was like.

    _____

    _____

Imagine that you want to learn more about identifying animal tracks that you see in the woods. After searching the Internet, you come up with the list of Web sites. Match the sites to the following statements.

6. You could learn how to track cats here.

    _____

7. This site shows you how to make a cast of animal tracks.

    _____

8. You can find Bigfoot information here.

    _____

9. This Web site lists three animals as leaving the most commonly seen tracks.

    _____

A. (*www.trail-trekking.net*) Commonly seen tracks: fox, squirrel, deer

B. (*www.cat-tracks.org*) The following might be helpful to anyone interested in identifying cat tracks.

C. (*www.jones-farm.net*) February's Nature Report: This month you can identify and make casts of some animal tracks.

D. (*www.big-foot.net*) Track the legendary Bigfoot.

Finding the Cause and Effect

There are times when one event causes another event to happen. Recognizing the **cause** (the reason) and the **effect** (the result) of a story event helps you better understand a story.

Example: Margaret fell from her tree house and broke her arm.
"Fell from her tree house" is the cause, and "broke her arm" is the effect.

Complete the following sentences by filling in the blanks with causes and effects from the box.

snow and ice	was not picking up dirt	worked all night
too much detergent	battery was dead	lighting their campfire
practicing for weeks	was very old	forgot an ingredient

1. Drew left the car's lights on overnight, and when Dad tried to start the car in the morning, the _____ .

2. Mom put _____ in the dishwasher, and when she came to unload it, there was foam all over the kitchen floor.

3. The employees of the electric company _____ restoring electricity to the city because of yesterday's high winds.

4. The house on the hill _____ and needed many repairs before it could be opened as a restaurant.

5. Main Street had a lot of potholes because of all of the _____ during last winter.

6. When Dad opened the vacuum cleaner to see why it _____ _____ , he found a tissue blocking the air passage.

7. Because of all of the rain, the campers had a difficult time _____ _____ .

8. The bread did not rise, because Alice _____ .

9. Jim was thrilled when he made the tennis team because he had been _____ _____ .

It's a Match!

Fill in the chart below by matching the causes and effects.

The regular path was blocked by a fallen tree.

Fishing in the stream was difficult.

It was easy for the blue team to score.

The batter hit a home run into the stands.

The water was running very fast.

The red team's goalie was out of position.

The pitcher threw a high ball.

John's horse bucked and threw him from the saddle.

The hikers took a longer route.

When the car backfired, it made a loud sound.

I hit golf balls at the practice range.

I had my best golf score.

Cause	Effect
A stray dog kept trying to eat our food.	We moved our picnic to a table.
1.	
2.	
3.	
4.	
5.	
6.	

Summer Bridge Reading RB-904095

That's a Fact!

> A **fact** is true. It can be proven.
>
> **Example:**   Leonardo da Vinci painted the *Mona Lisa*.
>
> An **opinion** is something that a person believes. An opinion cannot be proven.
>
> **Example:**   Leonardo da Vinci is the greatest artist of all time.

Write *F* next to each sentence that states a fact. Write *O* next to each sentence that states an opinion.

_____ **1.**   Utah, Arizona, New Mexico, and Colorado form the Four Corners in the United States.

_____ **2.**   The Eiffel Tower is the most amazing structure ever built.

_____ **3.**   The Eiffel Tower has 1,665 steps and stands 324 meters high.

_____ **4.**   Denver is the capital of Colorado.

_____ **5.**   The best skiers in the United States live in Colorado.

_____ **6.**   Madrid is the capital of Spain, and it is the country's most populous city.

_____ **7.**   Howard Carter discovered the tomb of Tutankhamun in 1922.

_____ **8.**   Roller coasters are the best attractions at amusement parks.

_____ **9.**   Santa Fe, New Mexico, is the oldest capital city in the United States.

_____ **10.**   Georgia O'Keeffe's paintings of New Mexico are beautiful.

_____ **11.**   Niagra Falls is a great place to go on vacation.

_____ **12.**   Niagra Falls is the largest waterfall in North America.

_____ **13.**   The phenomenon called "the northern lights" is caused by the collision of electrically charged particles from the sun.

_____ **14.**   Viewing the northern lights is an experience that everyone should have.

_____ **15.**   Wood Buffalo National Park is the largest national park in Canada.

Summer Bridge Reading RB-904095   © Rainbow Bridge Publishing

Endangered Environments

Read the passages and write *F* next to each statement that is a fact. Write *O* next to each statement that is an opinion.

Many people consider the Great Barrier Reef to be one of the seven natural wonders of the world. It is the largest coral structure and the largest structure ever made by non-human organisms.

The Great Barrier Reef consists mostly of tiny creatures called polyps. Each polyp lives inside a hard, rocklike shell that we recognize as coral. The polyps join together to create large forests of colorful coral in interesting shapes, such as fan, antler, and brain. When the polyp dies, the rocklike shell remains and another polyp grows on top of the dead one.

The fragile reef is constantly changing its shape and color. These changes are caused by many factors, including the polyps' constant activities. People visiting the reef can damage it through pollution and carelessness. Harmful animals and changes in the environment can also damage the reef.

_____ **1.** The tiny animals that make the Great Barrier Reef are called polyps.

_____ **2.** People should not be allowed to visit the reef.

_____ **3.** It is a good thing that there are so many polyps.

_____ **4.** The Great Barrier Reef is the largest coral structure in the world.

Tropical rain forests lie near the equator. In rain forests, rain falls almost every day and there is little variation in temperature. Tropical rain forests are packed with vegetation, including trees, vines, shrubs, and brightly colored flowers. About half of the world's species of plants and animals live in tropical rain forests.

The world's tropical rain forests are in great danger. They are being cut down to provide timber and firewood and to make room for homes, roads, farms, and factories. Some areas are being cleared for the mining of oil and valuable minerals. The habitats of thousands of species of plants and animals have already vanished. The way of life for many people who live in rain forests is also threatened by these changes.

_____ **5.** There is too much vegetation in the rain forests.

_____ **6.** Tropical rain forests are wet.

_____ **7.** All development should stop in the tropical rain forests.

_____ **8.** A tropical rain forest is a densely packed area of trees and plants.

Summer Bridge Reading RB-904095

You Decide

A **fictional** story is a story that someone imagined. Fictional stories may be based on some real experiences, but they are mostly made-up. **Nonfiction** stories are works that are not fiction. Stories about factual, documented events are nonfiction. A **biography**, which is a written account of another person's life, is a type of nonfiction.

Decide in which kind of stories each event would be found. Write *F* for fiction, *NF* for nonfiction, and *B* for biography.

_____ **1.** Most early Americans in the colonies wanted a government separate from England, and they fought for their freedom.

_____ **2.** Samuel Clemens grew up along the Mississippi River in Hannibal, Missouri.

_____ **3.** The Hershey Plant, the world's largest chocolate factory, is located in Hershey, Pennsylvania.

_____ **4.** After all of the visitors had left the zoo, the elephant put on his reading glasses and reached for a book.

_____ **5.** The ball rolled up to the boys and said, "If you want to play, I know some good games."

_____ **6.** George Washington Carver, who made more than 300 products from peanuts, went to Simpson College in Indianola, Iowa.

_____ **7.** The earthquake that disrupted the World Series in San Francisco occurred in 1989.

_____ **8.** Marla took pictures of the spacecraft when she visited the planet Delta Nine.

_____ **9.** The giraffe ducked its head way down to get into Trey's house.

_____ **10.** In 1932, Amelia Earhart became the first woman to fly nonstop across the Atlantic Ocean.

_____ **11.** When he was a boy, Richard lived in an enchanted castle with a horse, an owl, and a pair of friendly, talking pigs.

_____ **12.** In 1969, *Apollo 11* astronauts Neil Armstrong and "Buzz" Aldrin became the first men to walk on the moon.

Read the story and answer each question.

Nick Agrawal loved to listen to music. He had a large collection of CDs. As soon as he came home from school each day, he turned on his stereo. Nick was an excellent student, so his mother let him listen to music while he did his homework.

Nick's father was a judge. He worked long hours at the courthouse and came home very tired. In the evening, Nick's music bothered Mr. Agrawal. One day, Mr. Agrawal told Nick that he could no longer listen to his music after six o'clock in the evening. This was bad news for Nick, but he turned off his music.

1. How do you think Nick feels about turning off his music?

_____

2. What steps do you think Nick will take next?

_____

3. What does Nick do? (Read ahead and then, answer the question.)

_____

Nick wanted his father to be happy, but he also missed his rock music. He asked his father if it would be all right if he listened to his music with headphones. Nick's father agreed.

As soon as dinner was over, Nick put on his headphones. He washed the dishes while wearing his headphones. He did his homework while listening to his music that no one else could hear. This worked out well for everyone.

One day, Nick's father asked him a question about his homework. Nick did not hear his father because he was wearing his headphones. Mr. Agrawal grew angry. The headphones made Nick seem like he wasn't interested in the rest of the family. Mr. Agrawal told him that he could not listen to music while he did his homework. Nick was unhappy, but he turned off his music.

4. How do you think Nick feels about turning off his music?

_____

5. What steps do you think Nick will take next?

_____

6. What does Nick do? (Read ahead and then, answer the question.)

_____

Nick continued to listen to music with headphones while he did the dishes and other chores. One day, as Nick reached to put away some clean dishes, his headphone cord got caught on the silverware drawer. The cord jerked across Nick's arm, and he dropped the dishes that he was holding. They broke all over the floor.

Mr. and Mrs. Agrawal came running into the kitchen. When they learned what had happened, they decided to take the headphones away from Nick. Nick finished the dishes in silence.

Nick loved music so much that he felt he must listen to something. He proposed to his parents that he be allowed to listen to his own music in his room until dinnertime. After dinner, they could turn on a type of music that everyone would enjoy. Mr. and Mrs. Agrawal knew that music was important to Nick, so they agreed.

7. How does Nick handle the problem?

_____

8. Do you think Nick's parents do the right thing?

_____

9. What do you think will happen the next day?

_____

10. What is your favorite type of music? _____

11. When do you listen to music?_____

12. Are there any rules about music in your home? If so, describe them. If not, write about another rule that you have in your home.

_____

_____

_____

_____

Summer Bridge Reading RB-904095

The Riverdale Patriots

Read the story.

John's soccer team was called the Riverdale Patriots. He had been the captain of the team last year, and he wanted to be the captain one more year before he left middle school. Sam, John's best friend, had been cocaptain. The team had been really good last year. Sam and John hoped that the team would be as good or better this year.

One day, Sam called John and told him that something had happened. He explained that Mr. Stevens, their coach, was not going to be able to coach the team anymore. John could not believe the news. Sam told John that Mr. Stevens had been promoted in his company and that he would be traveling a lot during the soccer season. Mr. Stevens felt that this schedule would be unfair to the team.

The boys were really disappointed. They tried thinking of other players who had moms or dads who knew about soccer. Finally, John suggested calling Andy's uncle, Mr. Barber. He was a huge fan and was always at the Patriots' games. He had even played soccer in college.

"You know, coaching is just a volunteer kind of job. We can't be angry with Mr. Stevens," said John. "He was a great coach. It will be tough without Coach Stevens, but we should respect his need to stop coaching."

"Yeah, you're right. Let's call the community recreation department and tell them about our idea of asking Mr. Barber to help the Patriots," John said.

The boys headed for Sam's house to call the center to suggest their idea. Sam's mom was cooking dinner in the kitchen when the boys arrived. They explained their problem to Mrs. Sanders and tried calling the community recreation department. The secretary said that the team had already been assigned a new coach. The new coach of the Riverdale Patriots would be Jim Barber. The boys cheered and started jumping in the air, slapping hands, and shouting. They were going to have another great season.

The Riverdale Patriots

Write *T* next to each of the following statements that is true. Write *F* next to each of the following statements that is false. Refer to the passage (page 60) if necessary.

1. _____ Sam and John were on different soccer teams last year.

2. _____ Mr. Stevens is not going to be their coach this year.

3. _____ Sam's uncle is Jim Barber.

4. _____ Mr. Stevens' new job involves a lot of travel.

5. _____ The team is operated by the community boys club.

Answer the following questions using complete sentences.

6. Why do you think the boys want to find a new coach for their team?

_____

_____

_____

_____

7. From the information given in the story, how do you think the boys feel about Mr. Stevens after they hear the news?

_____

_____

_____

_____

Summer Bridge Reading RB-904095

Sailing in a Storm

Read the story below.

Tina and her dad loved to go sailing together. One summer, they decided to sail to Beaver Island. They put the boat in the water in Charlevoix, Michigan, at around six o'clock on a Thursday evening. They planned to dock the boat, shop, eat in town, and then set out for the island in the morning. Unfortunately, the marina did not have any available docks for their boat. They had no choice but to motor across the lake to the island that night.

Mr. Peterson and Tina motored the 23-foot sailboat through the channel and into Lake Michigan. It was a quiet evening. The sky was clear, and there was no wind. Mr. Peterson put up the sails, but they just flopped lightly in the calm air. The motor pushed them across the wide water. They listened to music and ate cheese-and-avocado sandwiches.

Around ten o'clock, the wind picked up suddenly. They turned off the motor and sailed with the brisk wind. Very quickly, the wind grew too strong and the waves became large. The small boat leaned and moved quickly through the water as the wind filled the sails.

When water started splashing into the boat, Mr. Peterson shouted, "We have to take down the sails! I can't handle this much wind!" Tina was scared. Her dad wanted her to go on deck to take down the sails. She was afraid that a wave might wash her overboard or that she might lose her balance. She decided to stay back and steer the boat instead, but Tina didn't like that either. It was hard to control the boat in the strong wind.

Mr. Peterson went on deck to take down the sails. Tina was shivering. The cold water was soaking her each time the boat crashed through a wave. She was shaking more from fear than cold. What would she do if her dad fell into the water? She didn't think that she could turn the boat around to get him. She wondered if they would ever make it to the island.

Once Mr. Peterson had tied up the sails, he took over the steering. Soon, the waves grew smaller, the wind died down, and several stars appeared in the sky as the clouds moved away. They motored ahead in silence.

When the island came into sight, Tina sat on the bow of the boat and gazed at it. She thought nothing had ever looked as beautiful as the island with its sheltered bay. They anchored the boat in the bay and put up a mooring light. They unrolled their sleeping bags inside the cabin and quickly fell asleep.

Sailing in a Storm

Answer the following questions about the passage (page 62).

1. Do you think that Tina and her dad have been sailing before this trip? Explain your answer.

   _____

   _____

2. How do you think Tina and her dad feel when they have to sail to the island that night? Explain your answer.

   _____

   _____

3. When they start out, there is no wind. How do you think that makes them feel?

   _____

4. When the wind begins to pick up, what do Tina and her dad do?

   _____

5. When the wind becomes too strong, they have a choice to make. What is that choice, and what do they choose to do?

   _____

6. What makes Tina shiver?_____

7. After the storm calms down, Tina and Mr. Peterson do not talk. Why do you think they are so quiet?

   _____

8. Why does the island look so beautiful to Tina?_____

9. What do you think they will do in the morning? _____

10. What sounds do you think you would hear in a storm on the lake?

    _____

    _____

Accessories

Drawing conclusions means considering the information you have and using that information to come up with answers that have not been directly stated.

Example: We saw one of the zookeepers training an animal that swims and lives on the rocks in one of the zoo's ponds. This animal was learning to balance a ball on its nose. Was it a tiger, a monkey, a giraffe, or a seal?

Conclusion: The animal is not a tiger, monkey, or giraffe because those animals do not swim or live in a zoo pond. So, the answer is *seal*.

Circle the letter in front of the clothing accessory described in each paragraph below. Then, underline the clue(s) that helped you decide.

1. Sharon was looking for something to carry her belongings on her business trip. She wanted it to be large enough to hold her money, glasses, address book, and a small cosmetic bag. She wanted it to have a shoulder strap and go with all of the clothes that she would be taking.

   A. wallet   **B.** purse   **C.** suitcase   **D.** backpack

2. Sharon went to buy something that she could wear after work. She knew how hot Florida could get in the summer, and she wanted to be able to cool off and relax at the beach after work. She found the perfect thing. It was light blue with little yellow fish that looked like they were swimming around each leg opening.

   A. beach towel   **B.** tennis shorts   **C.** bathing suit   **D.** golf shirt

3. Sharon stopped at a store. She told the salesman where she would be going, what clothes she would be taking, and how she would be on her feet a lot. She explained how she would like everything to match but that the most important thing was for her to be comfortable when she was standing all day and demonstrating her product. Sharon sat down to try on some of the things that the salesman brought her.

   A. hat   **B.** shoes   **C.** luggage   **D.** belt

Occupations

Read the descriptions of the characters. Circle the letter in front of their occupations. Then, explain why you made your selections.

1. Adam usually sits at a desk in the front of the office. He answers phones, makes appointments for clients, and greets them when they enter the law office. His appearance is important to his job because Adam is the first person whom people see when they come into the office.

   A. administrative assistant   **B.** lawyer   **C.** receptionist   **D.** telephone operator

   Why did you select that profession?_____

   _____

2. Jill never knows what to expect when she goes to work. Some days, she just patrols her route. Other days, the dispatcher radios her, telling her to go to a specific address to handle some trouble.

   A. chauffeur   **B.** police officer   **C.** firefighter   **D.** dog catcher

   Why did you select that profession?_____

   _____

3. Grant does not have an office, but he goes to work every day. He works in a tall building where he always has something to do for the good of the building. He might fix an out-of-order elevator or replace a pipe.

   A. maintenance man   **B.** janitor   **C.** plumber   **D.** electrician

   Why did you select that profession?_____

   _____

4. Tobie loves her work. On days she does not have surgery, Tobie might see as many as 40 patients. Many of them come for yearly checkups and shots. But sometimes, they are sick. Tobie cannot always tell what is wrong from a temperature reading or from listening to a patient's heartbeat. Tobie sometimes has to get more information about the patient's symptoms from the person to whom the patient belongs.

   A. dentist   **B.** surgeon   **C.** veterinarian   **D.** medical doctor

   Why did you select that profession?_____

   _____

Frozen in Time

Read the passage below.

For over 2,400 years, the body of a Siberian woman lay under the plains of the Ukok Plateau in Russia, frozen in a huge block of ice. The ice kept her body preserved until 1993, when a team of archaeologists carefully excavated the grave.

The archaeologists named the woman "The Ice Maiden." She had been a member of the Pazyryk culture. The Pazyryk people were hunters, sheepherders, and artists who lived from the sixth to the second century B.C.E. The Ice Maiden's grave was full of amazing finds, including six horses wearing elaborate harnesses. The archaeologists believe that the woman owned the horses. They think that the horses were killed during the Ice Maiden's funeral and then lowered into her grave.

Imagine how careful you would be if you were digging for a treasure that was over 2,400 years old. Archaeologists uncovered the woman slowly so that they wouldn't damage anything they found. When they reached the Ice Maiden's coffin, they pulled four copper nails from the lid. Inside, they found another two feet of ice. It took three days to melt it by pouring cupfuls of hot water on it. The melting ice revealed the body of an ancient woman. First, they saw her jawbone with flesh that looked like leather still on it. Next, the Ice Maiden's left shoulder came into view. On her shoulder was a blue tattoo of a mystical creature. She had another tattoo on her thumb, and one on her wrist that looked like a deer.

The Ice Maiden was 5½ feet (1.7 m) tall, which would have been tall for her time. She had beads wrapped around her wrists and a tall, decorated headdress on her head. She was wrapped in animal fur and dressed in a long robe. Beneath this, she wore a silk top and a white-and-maroon striped wool skirt. In the crook of her knee lay a red cloth case that held a small hand mirror. Pieces of gold foil speckled the area around her body.

Beside the woman stood a table. It held mutton (sheep's meat) and a slab of horse meat with a bronze knife sticking out of it. It was a Pazyryk tradition to place a meal with the person being buried. The archaeologists also found a stone dish with coriander seeds on it. Coriander is a fragrant herb that the Pazyryk people burned to mask unwanted odors.

The things that the archaeologists found fit together like pieces of a puzzle that made a picture of what life was like for the ancient ice woman. Archaeologists even looked at the food inside the horses' stomachs to see what clues they might find. In addition to half-digested pine needles, grass, and twigs, the scientists found bug larvae. Using these clues, scientists determined that the Ice Maiden's funeral had been held in the spring.

Archaeologists were able to discover that the Ice Maiden died of natural causes at about the age of 25. The whole community probably took part in her funeral, surrounding her body with all kinds of treasures. Each treasure held a secret that whispered to archaeologists, telling them just who this ancient woman was.

Frozen in Time

Answer the following questions.

1. What did archeologists do to melt the ice around the body of the woman?

_____

_____

What do you think about the way they did this?

_____

2. In your opinion, what are the three most interesting things that archaeologists found in the Ice Maiden's burial chamber?

_____   _____   _____

3. Imagine that you are an archaeologist and have the chance to go on a dig to discover something. What kind of discovery would you like to make?

_____

_____

4. Every piece of writing has a purpose. What do you think the purpose of this story is?

_____

Match each type of writing with its purpose.

_____ **5.** a newspaper article about a new movie

_____ **6.** a book about how to collect stamps

_____ **7.** a comic book

_____ **8.** a telephone book

_____ **9.** an Internet pop-up advertisement

_____ **10.** *The Lord of the Rings*

_____ **11.** a biography about a movie star

A. explains how to do something

B. entertains you while you read

C. gives an opinion about something

D. gives you phone numbers

E. encourages you to buy something

F. gives you information about someone's life

G. tells a story with illustrations

Summer Bridge Reading RB-904095

Emilio's Tadpoles

Read the story.

Emilio sat cross-legged by the dusty window. He stared at the foggy eucalyptus woods, wishing he were back in New Mexico playing air hockey with Carlos and José.

His family had moved to Santa Barbara, California, in January. He hadn't made a single friend in the two months since his family had moved there. He felt selfish being sad. Everyone else in his family was happy.

His five-year-old sister, Nadia, found a kitten in the woods, and his mom let her keep it. His father had a great new job at the television station. He loved talking about all of the people he met. His mom ran on the beach every morning and took classes at the community college in the afternoon.

Emilio didn't know what to do. None of the boys in his class lived nearby, and they all had known each other since kindergarten. Emilio was an outsider. The boys were polite enough, even friendly in a distant way, but after they said hello in the morning, they wandered off in groups that never included him. Emilio couldn't blame them. He and his old friends in New Mexico had done the same thing many times.

Emilio decided to stop feeling sorry for himself. Friends or no friends, it was a perfect Saturday afternoon. He opened the balcony door. He felt better as soon as he was outside. The tall, shaggy-barked trees smelled spicy in the damp sea air.

He ran down the back stairs two at a time. A carpet of feather-shaped fallen leaves cushioned his steps as he hurried down the familiar path. He was surprised when he got to the creek. No water tumbled over the rocks. Small, stagnant ponds dotted the dry bed.

When he looked more carefully into one of the pools, Emilio noticed that it was teeming with tiny, dark swimmers. They were so close together that they could hardly move. They were tadpoles. A few had back legs, but they were not yet ready to live on land. Unfortunately, the remaining water was evaporating fast. Suddenly, Emilio understood why everyone on the news had been talking about the drought.

Emilio couldn't make it rain, but he could help some of the tadpoles. He hurried back to the house to get a plastic bucket.

Extra! How could the tadpoles help Emilio make friends? Write what you think

will happen next. _____

_____

_____

Emilio's Tadpoles

Read each pair of sentences. Write *cause* or *effect* on each line.

1. Emilio's family moved. _____

   Emilio missed his friends Carlos and José. _____

2. Emilio's sister was happy. _____

   She had been allowed to have a kitten. _____

3. Emilio's mother was taking classes at the community college. _____

   She was learning new things. _____

4. Emilio's father got a job at the TV station. _____

   He met new people. _____

5. Emilio decided to walk to the creek. _____

   He was feeling sad and lonely. _____

6. There was a drought. _____

   There was not much water in the creek. _____

7. The water was evaporating fast. _____

   The tadpoles would not have enough time to change into frogs. _____

8. Emilio ran to the house to get a plastic bucket. _____

   He wanted to save some of the tadpoles. _____

Extra! Read the cause. Write a possible effect.

Cause: Emilio gave some of the tadpoles a safe place to live.

Effect: _____

Summer Bridge Reading RB-904095

A Surprise for Krysia

Read the story.

Magda waved to Krysia from across the crowded dirt street.

"Come," Magda called. "I have something to show you."

Krysia looked back at the dilapidated apartment building. Her four brothers were still at the factory, and her mother, in their tiny room on the second floor, was busy mending clothes. Krysia knew that nobody would miss her if she didn't stay away too long. She dodged two delivery wagons and a buggy to catch up with her friend. One of the horses whinnied and snorted at her.

"What is it?" Krysia asked in Polish.

"Speak only English. I want to learn," her friend said. She was already hurrying down the street, dodging men and women in dark, tattered clothes who chattered to each other in five different languages.

"Where are we going?" Krysia asked, breathless.

"I cannot tell you. I want it to be—how do they say—a surprise. Come." She cut down an alley between two tenements. A woman was hanging her laundry on a line above them. She waved. "Where are you girls going?" she asked.

"To the Settlement House," Magda called.

"Oh, yes! I have been there. That Miss Jane Addams is an angel," the woman said.

"What is the Settlement House?" Krysia asked.

"You will see," Magda said. "We are almost there."

They stepped out of the alley, crossed another street, and stood in front of a large, brick house.

Krysia hesitated. "It looks like a home of bad spirits," she said.

Magda laughed. "Some people who lived here thought it was. They kept a bucket of water so that the ghosts would not come down from the attic. Do not worry. If any spirits are in the house, they are happy." She led the way through the big door and up a flight of stairs.

Krysia followed, her eyes wide with wonder. Inside, the Settlement House was like a palace. There were plush rugs on the floor and paintings on the walls.

In a sunny room upstairs, paper, paints, and brushes were laid out on a table. A gorgeous bouquet of red and white roses was set up by the window. "I see you have brought a friend today, Magda," a smiling woman said.

"This is Krysia," Magda said.

"Welcome, Krysia," the woman said gently. "You may call me Miss Jane. Would you like to paint a picture of the flowers?" She handed Krysia a brush.

A Surprise for Krysia

Read the words in the box. Write the correct word on each line to complete each sentence.

spirit	tenement	chatter	bouquet
whinny	flight	palace	Settlement
plush	tattered	mending	laundry
gorgeous	delivery	dilapidated	

1. Magda and Krysia see a _____ of roses.

2. The two girls climb a _____ of stairs.

3. They go to the _____ House.

4. The apartment building is dirty and _____ .

5. The horses neigh and _____ .

6. A _____ is a shoddy apartment building.

7. Horses pull _____ wagons.

8. Worn-out clothes are _____ .

9. People laugh and _____ .

10. A woman hangs shirts and other _____ on the line.

11. Inside, the Settlement House seems like a _____ to Krysia.

12. Rugs that are thick and soft are _____ .

13. Another word for beautiful is _____ .

14. Another word for ghost is _____ .

15. Krysia's mother is _____ the clothes.

A Surprise for Krysia

Read "A Surprise for Krysia" (page 70). The story takes place in Chicago, Illinois, in the early 1900s. Fill in the circles to tell when each event or action took and/or takes place.

		Then	Now	Both
1.	People ride in buggies.	○	○	○
2.	Some children like art.	○	○	○
3.	People live in apartments.	○	○	○
4.	Some people speak Polish in America.	○	○	○
5.	There are cars.	○	○	○
6.	Horse-pulled wagons deliver groceries.	○	○	○
7.	Immigrants to the United States come from many countries.	○	○	○
8.	Jane Addams starts the Settlement House.	○	○	○
9.	Women hang laundry between buildings.	○	○	○
10.	People work in factories.	○	○	○
11.	Some people are poor.	○	○	○
12.	Chicago is a busy city.	○	○	○
13.	Some people help other people.	○	○	○
14.	People hang paintings on walls.	○	○	○

Extra! Read *A Personal Tour of Hull-House (How It Was)* by Laura Bufano Edge, (Lerner Publishing Group, 2001).

A Surprise for Krysia

Read "A Surprise for Krysia" (page 70). Circle the letter next to the word that completes each sentence.

1. Magda and Krysia are from
   A. Mexico.
   B. China.
   C. Poland.

2. Magda and Krysia are
   A. poor.
   B. rich.
   C. old.

3. The name of the woman who started the Settlement House is
   A. Susan B. Anthony.
   B. Jane Addams.
   C. Ann Sullivan.

4. One thing that children can do at the Settlement House is
   A. scrub floors.
   B. study art.
   C. cook.

5. The Settlement House is
   A. a new building.
   B. an old mansion.
   C. an office tower.

6. The language that Magda and Krysia speak best is
   A. English.
   B. Polish.
   C. Italian.

7. Their neighborhood is
   A. almost deserted.
   B. very wealthy.
   C. very crowded.

8. When it rains, the streets are probably
   A. muddy.
   B. dry.
   C. oily.

Extra! What might happen if Krysia takes her painting home? Write an ending for the story.

_____

_____

_____

_____

The Case of the Missing Heirloom

Read the story.

Dylan waited on the playground in the shade of a big cottonwood. If the other members of the Mystery Society didn't show up soon, he would have to meet the new client alone.

Then, he saw Ryan and Madison running across the yard. Ryan reached him first. "Sorry," Ryan gasped. "We just got back from the field trip."

"Our bus had a flat tire," Madison added. She was bent over trying to catch her breath.

"OK, well, we should get started," Dylan said. He led the way. "I got an e-mail this morning from a new boy in the neighborhood. He's in my little brother's class. He has a problem, and he needs our help."

"Great!" said Madison. "We haven't had a case all month."

"Actually, we haven't had a case since last year," Ryan said.

Madison shrugged. "So, who's keeping track?" she asked.

Dylan stopped in front of a two-story house that had once been white. He pulled a piece of paper out of his pocket and checked the address. "This is it," he said. The other two followed him up the weed-choked path to the door. Dylan knocked. There was no answer at first, so he knocked again, harder. The big door opened slowly, revealing a small boy in a red-striped T-shirt and jeans.

"Are you the Mystery Society?" he asked.

"That's us," said Dylan. "I'm Dylan, and these are my associates, Ryan and Madison. May we come in?"

"Sure," the boy said to Dylan. "I'm Joshua, but everybody calls me Josh." He led them to a small TV room and closed the door.

"What's the problem, Josh?" Dylan asked.

"I lost my grandfather's watch," Josh said. He looked as though he were going to cry. "If my mom finds out, I don't know what she'll do. It was worth a lot of money."

"It's okay, Josh. We'll help you find it," said Madison gently.

"When did you see it last?" asked Ryan.

"I saw it the day after we moved. It was in the top drawer of my bureau. When I looked for it yesterday, it was gone," Josh said.

"Let's go take a look," said Dylan.

Josh took them upstairs to his room and pointed to the bureau. Dylan and Ryan asked Josh more questions. Madison took the top drawer all of the way out. She reached into the space where the drawer had been. Triumphantly, she pulled out the watch.

The Case of the Missing Heirloom

Circle the letter next to each correct answer.

1. How does Josh hear about the Mystery Society?
   A. from Dylan's brother
   B. from Madison
   C. from the school newspaper

2. What does Josh lose?
   A. an antique fountain pen
   B. his grandfather's watch
   C. 10 dollars

3. How does Josh contact the club?
   A. by telephone
   B. by letter
   C. by e-mail

4. Why are Ryan and Madison late?
   A. They have to clean their rooms.
   B. Their teacher makes them stay late.
   C. Their bus has a flat tire.

5. Why does Josh close the door?
   A. He doesn't want the room to get cold.
   B. He wants to watch television.
   C. He doesn't want his mother to hear.

6. Who solves the mystery?
   A. Ryan
   B. Madison
   C. Josh

Summer Bridge Reading RB-904095   © Rainbow Bridge Publishing

The Case of the Missing Heirloom

Find each of the following **boldfaced** words in the story. Circle each correct answer.

1. The word **triumphant** means
   A. miserable.
   B. disappointed.
   C. victorious.

2. When Madison **shrugs**, she moves her
   A. shoulders.
   B. head.
   C. fingers.

3. A **cottonwood** is a
   A. car.
   B. tree.
   C. animal.

4. An **heirloom** is
   A. something inherited.
   B. a brush.
   C. something on which to weave.

5. A **client** is
   A. a detective.
   C. a student.
   C. a customer.

6. A **society** is
   A. a club.
   B. a house.
   C. a game.

7. If the path is **weed-choked**, the yard needs
   A. to be weeded and trimmed.
   B. a new fountain.
   C. a dog.

8. The word **associates** means
   A. enemies.
   B. fellow workers.
   C. students.

9. If you **gasp**, you are trying to
   A. pick up something.
   B. catch your breath.
   C. hold something.

10. A **bureau** is
    A. a shed used for storage.
    B. a dresser.
    C. a group of detectives.

Extra! Fill in the missing word:

Triumphant is to defeated as happy is to _____.

Summer Bridge Reading RB-904095

The Case of the Missing Heirloom

Read each statement. Circle the letter next to the sentence from "The Case of the Missing Heirloom" (page 70) that shows the statement is true.

1. Josh's house needs a lot of work.

   A. "It was in the top drawer of my bureau."

   B. Dylan stopped in front of a two-story house that had once been white.

2. Dylan does not go on the field trip.

   A. "Sorry," Ryan gasped. "We just got back from the field trip."

   B. "Great!" said Madison. "We haven't had a case all month."

3. Josh is younger than Dylan.

   A. "He's in my little brother's class."

   B. "I saw it the day after we moved."

4. Josh's house has two stories.

   A. She reached into the space where the drawer had been.

   B. Josh took them upstairs to his room and pointed to the bureau.

5. Josh has not told his mother that the watch is missing.

   A. "It was worth a lot of money."

   B. "If my mom finds out, I don't know what she'll do."

6. Dylan knows how to use a computer.

   A. "I got an e-mail this morning from a new boy in the neighborhood."

   B. Dylan and Ryan asked Josh more questions.

Extra! Answer this riddle if you can: I have two hands but no arms. I have a band with no trumpets or drums. I keep something that most people are always trying to save.

What am I? _____

The Case of the Missing Heirloom

Read each pair of sentences below. Write *C* next to the sentence that states the cause. Write *E* next to the sentence that states the effect.

1. _____ Madison and Ryan are late.

   _____ The bus has a flat tire.

2. _____ Josh needs help

   _____ Josh e-mails Dylan.

3. _____ Josh cannot find the watch.

   _____ The watch slips behind the drawer.

4. _____ Josh is afraid that his mother will be angry.

   _____ Josh loses his grandfather's watch.

5. _____ Dylan leads the way to the house.

   _____ Dylan has the address.

6. _____ The members of the Mystery Society are excited.

   _____ It is the Mystery Society's first case in a long time.

7. _____ Ryan and Madison run.

   _____ Ryan and Madison are late.

8. _____ The house has been empty for a while.

   _____ The house needs a lot of work.

9. _____ The bureau is in Josh's room.

   _____ Josh takes the Mystery Society upstairs.

Extra! Circle the event that probably happened first: the bus has a flat tire; Josh loses the watch; the Mystery Society meets for the first time, Josh moves.

Find Abe!

Read the story below.

When Danny came home from school, he tossed his books on the table.

"Abe!" he called. "Where are you, boy?"

His beagle did not come.

He cracked the door of his mom's office. She turned around. "Oh, hi, Danny. I didn't know you were home," she said.

"Have you seen Abe?" he asked.

"No," she said. "I let him out at lunchtime. I assumed that he came back in. Check in your room. Maybe he's just asleep."

"OK, thanks," Danny said. He checked the house from top to bottom. Abe was gone. When he told his mom, she was worried, too.

"I'll go out and search for him," Danny said. "Will you call the neighbors?"

"Good idea," his mom said, picking up the phone.

Danny walked down the street, calling toward every driveway, "Abe, come here, boy."

Soon, he saw neighbors from up and down the block climbing into their cars. When they drove by him, they waved. He could tell that they were looking, too.

Danny searched for over an hour. He was hungry and tired. His feet were sore. He decided to find out whether Abe had come home on his own.

He saw the crowd in his front yard from halfway down the block. Cars were parked in the middle of the street, and people were standing around. As he came closer, he noticed that a man he didn't recognize had a dog that looked like Abe on a leash. Mrs. Sildano from the apartment across the street was holding a dog that looked like Abe in her arms. Mr. Chan from next door was telling a dog that looked like Abe to sit, and Jenny from the house on the corner was tying a dog that looked like Abe to a fence post.

His mom was standing on the porch, talking on the phone. When she saw Danny, she waved her arms. "Help!" she called. "I don't know what to do."

Just then, the real Abe emerged from a private hiding place between the houses. He yawned and stretched. He trotted to each of the other Abes and wagged his tail, just to be friendly. When Abe came to Danny, he pawed the leg of Danny's jeans.

Danny's mom invited the neighbors to a party that weekend to thank them for their help. They were all glad that the real Abe was home. They hurried to take the other beagles back to where they found them.

Find Abe!

Read each pair of sentences below. Draw a line from each sentence to *cause* or *effect*.

1. Abe does not come.

Danny thinks that Abe is lost.

cause

effect

2. The neighbors look for Abe.

Danny's mom calls the neighbors.

cause

effect

3. Each neighbor thinks that they have found Abe.

Many beagles look similar.

cause

effect

4. All of the neighbors like Danny and Abe.

They go out to look for Abe.

cause

effect

5. The neighbors take the dogs back.

The real Abe comes out of his hiding place.

cause

effect

6. The street is crowded in front of the house.

All of the neighbors bring an Abe home.

cause

effect

7. The neighbors all help.

Danny's mom invites them to a party.

cause

effect

Extra! Answer this riddle if you can: I have knots, but I am not a rope. I have bark, but I am not a dog. I may even have a lot of rings.

What am I? _____

Summer Bridge Reading RB-904095

Javier's Bike

Read the story below.

Every boy on Javier's block had a bike. Javier wanted one, too. He watched his friends ride off to the park. They waved to him as they went by.

"Come on, Javier," they called.

He just waved back. It was three long blocks to the park. Walking was too slow. By the time he got there, it would be time to go home.

One night, Javier helped his mother with the dishes.

"Please," he said, "can I have a bike for my birthday?"

His mother gave him a plate to dry. "Your sister needs new shoes. Your grandfather in Mexico is sick. We have to send money for the doctor. I'm sorry, Javier. A bike costs too much. We will have a piñata for your birthday as we always do."

Javier went to his room. He did not want his mother to see how sad he was. He sat down on the bed and stared at the wall. How would he ever get a bike?

Then, he remembered something that he had heard in class. It was a saying. "Where there's a will, there's a way." It meant that you could find a way to get what you wanted. You just had to want it enough to keep trying.

The next day was Saturday. Javier was about to walk to the park when he saw Mrs. Martinez next door. She was pulling weeds in her garden. Mrs. Martinez was an old woman, and there were too many weeds for her to pull by herself. Her children all lived in other towns. They could not help her. Javier said that he would help. She smiled and told him to get some gloves. She pointed to a shed behind the house.

When Javier opened the door, he saw the gloves. He also saw a bike. It was old and the tires were flat, but it looked beautiful to Javier.

He heard a voice behind him. "That was my youngest son's bike," Mrs. Martinez said. "Do you like it?"

"Oh yes!" said Javier.

"Get the gloves and help me. When we finish, I will give you a cool drink," she said.

Javier picked up the gloves slowly. How could he have dreamed that the old woman would give him such a fine gift for such a little favor?

He turned around. Mrs. Martinez was smiling. "And the bike, of course," she said.

Answer the following questions about the passage (page 81).

1. What does Javier want, and why does he want it?

_____

_____

_____

_____

2. Why can't he get what he wants for his birthday?

_____

_____

_____

_____

3. Javier offers to help someone. Who is it, and why does he want to help?

_____

_____

_____

_____

4. How does Javier get what he wants?

_____

_____

_____

_____

Extra! Practice summarizing. On an extra sheet of paper, tell the story of your favorite movie in your own words.

The Daring Young Man in the Vin Fiz

Read the passage.

In 1903, two brothers who owned a bicycle shop, Orville and Wilbur Wright, designed, built, and flew the first airplane. Before they built their twin-winged Flyer, the Wright brothers studied the work of other aeronautic pioneers.

They probably learned about another pair of brothers, Joseph and Jacques Montgolfier, who invented the first working hot air balloon in 1783. They certainly read about gliders designed by inventors such as George Cayley and Otto Lilienthal. They also studied the work of Samuel P. Langley, who built a series of powered gliders, called Aerodromes, throughout the 1890s.

By 1911, the Wrights and other adventurous people were testing the capabilities of their new "aeroplane." A famous publisher, William Randolph Hearst, offered a challenge to these daredevils. He said that he would give $50,000 to the first person who flew from coast to coast in the United States in 30 days or fewer.

Calbraith Perry Rodgers decided to go for the prize. Six feet four inches tall and a former football star, Cal came from a family of military heroes. He could not go into the U.S. Navy because he was deaf. He had to find other ways to test his courage. He took flying lessons from Orville Wright and bought a Flyer. It was the first airplane that the brothers sold to a private individual. The plane was made of wood and stretched linen. It had no instruments. At full speed, it would fly 55 miles per hour.

Cal, charming and confident, convinced J. Ogden Armour, who owned a large company, to sponsor him. Armour's company manufactured a popular grape soft drink called Vin Fiz. Cal had an advertisement for the drink painted on the rudders and the undersides of the wings. In return, the company agreed to pay the aviator five dollars for every mile he flew.

Because of the plane's lack of instruments, Cal could not just take off and fly across the United States. He had to follow ground routes. The best transcontinental ground routes in 1911 were railroads. Cal arranged for a train to follow his flight. It carried his mechanic and had special cars with replacement parts and other support equipment. He needed the help. By the time he reached the West Coast, he had crashed at least 16 times. Only one rudder and a wing strut remained of the original plane; the rest had been replaced. He didn't win Hearst's prize, because his trip took 49 days, but Cal Rodgers did go down in history as the first person to fly across the United States.

The Daring Young Man in the Vin Fiz

Follow the directions to answer the questions. Refer to the passage (page 83) if necessary.

1. Which of the following reasons best explains why the author wrote "The Daring Young Man in the Vin Fiz?" Circle the letter next to the correct answer.

   A. to explain why Calbraith Perry Rodgers' plane was named the Vin Fiz

   B. to convince the reader to fly safely

   C. to provide information about the first cross-country flight in the United States

2. Circle the word that does not belong.

   balloon   glider   train   airplane

3. Read the following sentences. Write *C* on the line next to the sentence that states the cause. Write *E* on the line next to the sentence that states the effect.

   _____ The Wright brothers learned from the successes and failures of others.

   _____ The Wright brothers studied the work of other inventors.

4. Write a sentence that points out one way in which life in 1911 was similar to life today.

   _____

   _____

5. Cal Perry Rodgers and other early aviators used "the iron compass." What was it? Circle the letter next to the correct answer.

   A. a mountain with a large iron deposit

   B. railroad tracks

   C. a heavy compass on the airplane

Extra! List all of the dates in "The Daring Young Man in the Vin Fiz." Make a time line showing the events in the article. Search the Internet using the phrases "Vin Fiz," "Calbraith Perry Rodgers," and "history of flight" to learn more about this fascinating adventure.

The Lair of the High Cave Dragon

Read the story.

Prince Lazar urged on his horse through the dense woods. He had been riding for hours, and his horse was breathing hard. But the summons was urgent, and they were very close to the castle. The prince had already glimpsed bright banners through the trees.

Two knights in gleaming armor with red plumes on their helmets met him at the edge of the forest. They escorted him through the castle gates.

"Prince Lazar has arrived, your majesty," the first knight announced.

"Not a moment too soon," said the second knight, casting an accusatory glance in the prince's direction. The knights slipped out a side door, leaving the prince alone with the king.

"I came with all possible speed, your highness," said the prince with a bow.

"Yes, I know. Don't mind Sir Albert. He panics easily. Sir Percy will see to him." The king rose from his throne, walked over to a nearby table, and filled two silver goblets with cool spring water. He handed one to the prince and kept the other for himself.

"What is the challenge, sire?" the prince asked.

The king gestured for the prince to sit, and then, he sat down himself. "The High Cave Dragon emerged from his lair three nights ago. He caught the full moon resting on the edge of the sky and snatched it away for his treasure chest. Since then, no man, woman, or child in the kingdom has been able to sleep."

"Ah," said the prince, "no wonder Sir Albert was so disturbed. How shall I find the moon and restore it to its rightful place in the sky?"

The king looked at Lazar and paused. "You must take the goblet you now hold and carry it up Dragon Mountain." He pointed out the window toward a smoking peak on the distant horizon.

"Enter the lair at midday, when the dragon is sleeping. Capture the reflection of the moon in the water. Then, find a place to hide. The moment the sun goes down, toss the water toward the mountain's peak. The moon will chase its reflection. She will return to the sky, and we will all sleep again. I hesitate to ask this of you. The task is more perilous than it seems."

The prince bowed. "I leave at once, your majesty," he said.

85

The Lair of the High Cave Dragon

Circle the letter next to each correct answer.

1. Who is the hero of this story?
   A. the king
   B. Sir Percy
   C. Prince Lazar

2. What problem must the hero solve?
   A. He must return the moon to the sky.
   B. He must figure out why the king is not sleeping.
   C. He must find a magic ring.

3. What kind of story is this?
   A. mystery
   B. fantasy
   C. contemporary

4. Where does this story take place?
   A. in a make-believe kingdom
   B. in Hollywood
   C. on the moon

5. What is the second knight's name?
   A. Sir George
   B. Sir Albert
   C. Sir Lancelot

6. When does this story probably take place?
   A. now
   B. long ago
   C. in the future

Answer the following questions using complete sentences.

7. What clues helped you figure out who the hero of the story is?

   _____

   _____

8. How did you decide when the story takes place?

   _____

   _____

Extra! Read *Taran Wanderer* by Lloyd Alexander (Yearling Books, 1969).

Most work involving reference materials requires using the skill of **alphabetizing**. Dictionaries, encyclopedias, and other reference materials are organized alphabetically.

Sometimes, it is only necessary to look at the first letter when alphabetizing a list.

Example: banana   grapefruit   lime   peach

However, sometimes it is necessary to look at the second, third, or fourth letters when the first letter or letters are the same.

Example: shift   sign   slant   spot

Number the lists alphabetically.

A. _____ antilog   **B.** _____ most   **C.** _____ anchor   **D.** _____ contest

_____ antigen   _____ mosaic   _____ annex   _____ contact

_____ antic   _____ mosquito   _____ analyze   _____ contrary

_____ antique   _____ mosey   _____ anytime   _____ confusion

_____ antidote   _____ moss   _____ angel   _____ continue

Dictionary Skills

Guide words are the two words found at the top of each dictionary page. Use guide words to help you locate a word in a dictionary. Any entry word listed on that page will fall alphabetically between the two guide words.

Examples: engage—equal   happen—hassle   entrance—hardware

Circle the entry words that would be found on the dictionary pages with the guide words listed.

1.   report—resolve
require, restrain, resist, reply, reserve, represent

3.   pucker—put
push, pulley, public, pudding, purple, putt

2.   honor—howl
hover, hoist, honey, hound, hoop

4.   dice—digit
decide, diesel, differ, digital, digest, dictate

Using the Keys

When looking up information in reference materials, such as encyclopedias or almanacs, decide what question you are trying to answer. Write down the question and notice the **key words**, or the important words in the sentence. Looking up information about the key words will help you answer your question.

Examples: Under what circumstances did Harry <u>Truman</u> become president?
(When looking up a person, it is usually best to use the last name.)
Who was <u>Galileo</u>? (Some people are best known by their first names.)
Why did <u>Alexander Hamilton</u> and <u>Aaron Burr</u> duel?
(Sometimes, more than one reference or key word is given.)

Underline the key words in each question.

1. Who invented the printing press?

2. Where is Mount Rushmore located?

3. Who invented the radio and the phonograph?

4. What is ozone, and of what importance is it to the environment?

5. What kind of clothing did people wear in the late 1700s?

6. In what movie did Mickey Mouse first appear?

7. How was Harriet Tubman affiliated with the Underground Railroad?

8. In what country did croquet originate?

9. In what kind of climate does the cactus grow best?

10. What function does the liver have in your body?

11. Which animals are endangered, and what is being done to save them?

12. What foods are good sources of vitamin C?

13. What changes did the Industrial Revolution bring to America?

14. What is the history of political parties in England?

Encyclopedias

> An **encyclopedia** is a book or set of books containing information on various subjects. The subjects are organized alphabetically. On the outside of each book is a letter or letters that show alphabetically which subjects will be found inside the book. Encyclopedias also have guide words at the top of each page to help you locate the subjects inside.

Write the number(s) of the volume(s) in which you would look to find the answers to the questions.

A. _____ What kind of vegetation grows in the Arctic?

B. _____ From what country do pandas come, and what do they like to eat?

C. _____ On what continent is Luxembourg located?

D. _____ What was the first mode of transportation in the United States?

E. _____ What part did the Alamo play in Texas's history?

F. _____ What reptiles live in the United States, and what characteristics do they share?

G. _____ What is the difference between a tornado and a hurricane?

H. _____ What did Louis Pasteur invent?

I. _____ Who was president when the United States negotiated the Louisiana Purchase?

J. _____ What discoveries did Magellan make?

K. _____ Who were England's monarchs from William the Conqueror to the present?

L. _____ Who were the allies in World War II?

M. _____ What is the life cycle of salmon?

N. _____ Who were the Etruscans, and what were their accomplishments?

O. _____ When did printing begin, and how did it change culture?

Map It Out

> An **atlas** is a specialized reference book that includes a collection of maps. The maps may be of states, countries, or the world. Sometimes, an atlas includes informative tables or other factual matter. Some atlases are specialized. They might include maps of the night sky, rivers, or roadways.

Use the map of Missouri to answer the questions.

1. What is Missouri's capital?_____

2. How many states border Missouri? _____

3. Which states border Missouri on the west?_____

   _____

4. Which cities have three major highways going through them?_____

   _____

5. What river borders Missouri on the east? _____

6. Springfield is what direction from the capital?_____

7. What city is east of the capital? _____

Use the number and letter pairs below to identify the cities on the map by going across from the numbers and up from the letters.

8. 5, B

   _____

9. 2, C

   _____

10. 4, D

    _____

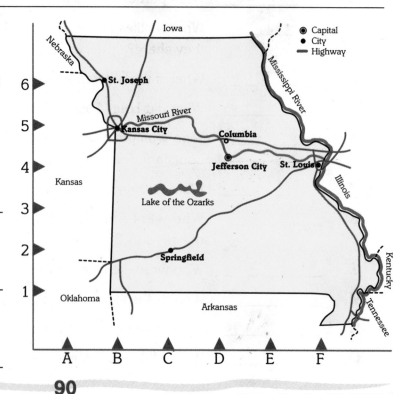

Summer Bridge Reading RB-904095

Staying on Topic

Jacy Bich

A **glossary** is a specialized dictionary. It is usually at the back of a specialized reference book and has words pertaining to only the subjects that are covered in the book. The words are arranged alphabetically, like in a dictionary.

Several words are listed together as they would be in a glossary. Decide what the subject of the book is. Then, underline the title of the book.

Example: Glossary: Akita, golden retriever, poodle, rottweiler
Book title: <u>Dogs as Pets</u>   Hunting Dogs   Miniature Dogs

1. hickory, maple, oak, sycamore
Wild Flowers   <u>Trees in Your Backyard</u>   Forest Lands

2. Lincoln Memorial, Pentagon, U.S. Capitol Building, White House
<u>Washington, D.C.</u>   Springfield, Illinois   Seattle, Washington

3. Argentina, Brazil, Chile, Venezuela
North American Countries   European Countries   <u>South American Countries</u>

4. arctic circle, equator, prime meridian, international date line
<u>Longitude and Latitude</u>   Traditional Landmarks   Places on a Street Map

5. baseball, basketball, football, hockey
Ball Games   <u>Competitive Team Sports</u>   Winter Games

6. Columbus, Ohio; Jefferson City, Missouri; Lincoln, Nebraska; Madison, Wisconsin
United States Cities   Cities Named for U.S. Presidents   <u>U.S. State Capitals</u>

7. heart, kidneys, liver, lungs
The Respiratory System   <u>Organs of the Body</u>   The Nervous System

8. Atlantic, New England, Northwest, Rocky Mountain
Western Universities   <u>Regions of the United States</u>   Midwestern Culture

9. Newton, Sir Isaac; Pasteur, Louis; Salk, Jonas; Van Allen, James
Twentieth Century Inventions   American Biographies   <u>Famous Scientists</u>

10. Apache, Cherokee, Iroquois, Navajo
America's Past   <u>American Indian Tribes</u>   America's European Beginnings

Looking It Up

The **table of contents** and the **index** in a book are directories. The table of contents is found in the front of a book. It lists each chapter by its title or subject. If a book has an index, it is at the end of the book. The index lists specific names and subjects in alphabetical order and the page or pages on which information about the names and subjects can be found.

Using the table of contents and index, write the chapter and page numbers on which you would look to answer the questions.

Table of Contents

Index

	Chapter	Page(s)
1. What things destroy ozone in the atmosphere?	_____	_____
2. What are the layers of the atmosphere?	_____	_____
3. What is ozone?	_____	_____
4. Are there solutions to the ozone problem?	_____	_____
5. What is the connection between ozone and cancer cells?	_____	_____

Summer Bridge Reading RB-904095

Where Would You Look?

When you have to look up something, you should first know precisely what you want to find out and then decide what sources would contain the information you need.

Circle the sources that you would use to locate the following information.

1. life in Russia under Joseph Stalin

   atlas   encyclopedia   dictionary   glossary

2. words in a book associated with computer science: *download*, *byte*, *RAM*, *Internet*

   dictionary   encyclopedia   glossary   table of contents

3. locations of the oceans of the world

   atlas   dictionary   index   glossary

4. desert wildlife

   index   table of contents   glossary   encyclopedia

5. definitions of spelling words: breezy, eldest, grateful, merry, oriental, stackable

   glossary   index   dictionary   table of contents

6. the chapter pertaining to French artists

   encyclopedia   dictionary   index   table of contents

7. pages relating to the constellations

   index   encyclopedia   glossary   dictionary

8. distance from Indianapolis, Indiana, to San Diego, California

   table of contents   index   atlas   glossary

9. definitions of words found in the second chapter of a science book

   encyclopedia   glossary   table of contents   index

10. military career of General George McClellan

    dictionary   glossary   atlas   encyclopedia

Answer Key

Page 10

```
a m u s e     c a m e     s t o p
d     n     x h     e     e
o   d r i v e     e   s p a r e
r     e   t     e k     a
e a r n   t u r n   c a r e s s
    l     e     g     r     a
t r a i l     d o u b t
e     r     y     r     e d g e
p r y   h e a l     e     v
l     e     a     b   s h
a l l o w   i m a g e   g u s h
i     l     d     e
n     l o n g     e
e v e r y         s t r o n g
```

Page 11

1. maize; 2. presence; 3. vein;
4. cruise; 5. medal; 6. beech;
7. stationary; 8. rite; 9. knead;
10. aisle; 11. lyre; 12. sealing

Page 12

1. morn, homophone; 2. few,
antonym; 3. ask, antonym; 4. safe,
synonym; 5. asleep, antonym;
6. peddle, homophone; 7. soiled,
synonym; 8. common, antonym

Page 13

1. lemon; 2. year; 3. aunt; 4. cow;
5. haul; 6. write; 7. sole; 8. up;
9. neck; 10. place; 11. stalk; 12. fish;
13. four; 14. vine; 15. transparent;
16. hungry; 17. pool; 18. mason;
19. court; 20. anatomy

Page 14

1. thoughtless; 2. closed; 3. accept;
4. brave; 5. rescue; 6. certain;
7. ferocious; 8. deposit; 9. biology;
10. typical; 11. decrease; 12. future

Page 15

1. food; 2. trunk; 3. water; 4. shower;
5. tusks; 6. upper; 7. enemies; 8. bore;
9. molars; 10. difficult; 11. wear;
12. replaced; 13. life; 14. longer;
15. usually

Page 16

1. not heavy; 2. without a saddle;
3. thin pieces of wood or plastic;
4. chest of drawers; 5. separate into

Page 16 (continued)

equal parts; 6. a graduated series of
notes; 7. proper; 8. lags

Page 17

1. produce; 2. wind; 3. moderate;
4. present; 5. record; 6. conduct

Page 18

1. mid<u>stream</u>, middle of the stream;
2. post<u>graduate</u>, a person continuing
their studies after graduation;
3. im<u>proper</u>, not proper; 4. uni<u>color</u>, one
color; 5. sub<u>zero</u>, below zero;
6. superhuman; 7. telescope;
8. subcategory; 9. immobilize;
10. midterm

Page 19

1. <u>contest</u>ant, a participant of a contest;
2. <u>leader</u>ship, quality of a leader;
3. <u>courage</u>ous, qualities of courage;
4. <u>sweet</u>ly, sweet manner;
5. <u>lobby</u>ist, someone who lobbies;
6. resident; 7. reddish; 8. specialist;
9. abruptly; 10. mechanical;
11. patiently; 12. carefully; 13. easily
14. generous; 15. timely

Page 20

1. S; 2. S; 3. S; 4. S; 5. M; 6. M; 7. M;
8. S; 9. S; 10. S; 11. M; 12. S; 13. M;
14. M; 15. S

Page 21

1. B.; 2. E.; 3. G.; 4. A.; 5. H.; 6. F.; 7. C.;
8. D.

Page 22

1. trophy: proudly stood; 2. clouds: spit;
3. Autumn leaves: danced; 4. Horns:
honked angrily; 5. sun: played; 6. clouds:
marched; 7. house: waited

Page 24

A. 5; B. 3; C. 10; D. 1; E. 7; F. 4; G. 9;
H. 2; I. 8; J. 6

Page 25

A. 2, 3, 1; B. 1, 3, 2; C. 3, 2, 1, 4;
D. 3, 1, 4, 2

Page 27

1. 2, 1, 4, 3; 2. B, D, A, C; 3. 6, 1, 2, 4,
3, 5

Page 28

1. B.; 2. C.; 3. C

Page 29

Answers will vary.

Page 30

A. 2, 1, 3; B. 3, 1, 2; C. 1, 3, 2;
D. 2, 3, 1; E. 3, 2, 1

Page 31

1. friendly; 2. eleven; 3. sweet;
4. rabbit; 5. beagle; 6. Travers;
7. Becky; 8. mean; 9. Preston;
10. Sunday; 11. Marty; 12. Shiloh

Page 32

1. China; 2. pizza; 3. four; 4. chopsticks

Page 34

First Paragraph

Main idea: Pioneers made temporary
houses because they had many tasks to
complete. Details: busy planting
gardens and crops, digging wells,
preparing for winter

Second Paragraph

Main idea: The pioneers made sod
houses. Details: not many trees
around, tough sod was thick with roots,
cut top layer of soil into bricks,
roots helped cement bricks together

Third Paragraph

Main idea: A well-made sod house was
comfortable and dry. Details: wooden
frames and glass for doors and windows,
roofs of straw and dirt or wood and
sod, stayed cool in summer and warm
in winter

Fourth Paragraph

Main idea: Unwanted animals lived with
the pioneers in the sod house.
Details: mice, snakes, insects

Fifth Paragraph

Main idea: Pioneers were strong,
determined people. Details: worked
hard, clever use of natural resources

Page 36

1. He injured and fought with other
players.; 2. He owned virtually every
hitting record.; 3. He was aggressive and
dominated them.; 4. The Georgia Peach;
Answers will vary.

Answer Key

Page 37

What would you like to have for dinner tonight? / Lasagna would be my first choice.; Have you counted the number of trees on the property? / Yes, there are 14 maples, 10 oaks, and 2 others that I don't recognize.; Have you read any of the *Harry Potter* books? / Yes, I read the first and second ones. They were both exciting.; What is your favorite rock band? / My favorite is Spaghetti. I love their music.; How many steps are there on the way to the top of the Washington Monument? / I read that there are 898. The monument is surrounded by 50 U.S. flags.; Did you see Potter running in the race around the lake? / Yes, Potter came in first place.

Page 38

1. Emily; 2. caring, resourceful; 3. Answers will vary.

Page 39

1. Billy and Roger; 2. helpful, studious;

Page 40

3. athletic, unfriendly; 4. considerate, appreciative

Page 41

1. impeached and removed; 2. one chief justice and eight associate; 3. several hundred; 4. interpret; 5. of national importance; 6. maintain the laws; 7. parties involved; 8. approved

Page 43

1. A. Asia, B. Africa, C. North America, D. South America, E. Antarctica, F. Europe, G. Australia; 2. 2,538 meters; 3. Nile and Amazon; 4. Australia and Europe; 5. Asia, Africa; 6. Everest, McKinley, and Aconcagua; 7. A. Volga, B. Murray-Darling, C. Missouri, D. Chang (Yangtze), E. Amazon, F. Nile

Page 44

A. 3, 2, 1 or 3, 1, 2; B. 2, 1, 3, 4; C. 3, 5, 1, 2, 4

Page 45

A. Drawing may vary, but should match directions.; B. honest; C. Drawing may vary, but should match directons.; D. yo-yos

Page 47

Limericks will vary.

Page 48

1. C.; 2. A.; 3. A.; 4. A.; 5. C.; 6. B.; 7. B.; 8. A.; 9. A.; 10. B.

Page 49

1. coffee; 2. pyramid; 3. Atlantic Ocean; 4. astronomy; 5. cats; 6. Siamese cats; 7. whales; 8. gutter; 9. disappointed; 10. neighbor; 11. yard; 12. certain; 13. green; 14. jeans; 15. nose; Extra: a rock

Page 50

Arabian Camel: one hump, trained for racing, shorter hair; Bactrian Camel: two humps, sturdier, can withstand cooler climates; Both: hump stores fat for food, sway when walk, used for food and clothing

Page 51

Extra: Answers will vary.

Page 52

1. Answers will vary.; 2. outside in a tree at night during winter. 3. gently like downy feathers; 4. Answers will vary.; 5. Answers will vary.; 6. B.; 7. C.; 8. D.; 9. A.

Page 53

1. battery was dead; 2. too much detergent; 3. worked all night; 4. was very old; 5. snow and ice; 6. was not picking up dirt; 7. lighting their campfire; 8. forgot an ingredient; 9. practicing for weeks

Page 54

Order of answers may vary.
1. cause—The regular path was blocked by a fallen tree. effect—The hikers took a longer route.; 2. cause—The water was running very fast. effect—Fishing in the stream was difficult.; 3. cause—The red team's goalie was out of position. effect—It was easy for the blue team to score.; 4. cause—The pitcher threw a high ball. effect—The batter hit a home run into the stands.; 5. cause—When the car backfired, it made a loud sound. effect—John's horse bucked and threw him from the saddle.; 6. cause—I hit golf

Page 54, (continued)

balls at the practice range. effect—I had my best golf score.

Page 55

1. F; 2. O; 3. F; 4. F; 5. O; 6. F; 7. F; 8. O; 9. F; 10. O; 11. O; 12. F; 13. F; 14. O; 15. F

Page 56

1. F; 2. O; 3. O; 4. F; 5. O; 6. F; 7. O; 8. F

Page 57

1. NF; 2. B; 3. NF; 4. F; 5. F; 6. B; 7. NF; 8. F; 9. F; 10. B; 11. F; 12. NF

Pages 58–59

1.–2. Answers will vary. 3. listen to his music on headphones. 4.–5. Answers will vary.; 6. listen to his parents.; 7. he offers a compromise.; 8.–12. Answers will vary.

Page 61

1. F; 2. T; 3. F; 4. T; 5. F; 6.–7. Answers will vary.

Page 63

1.–3. Answers will vary.; 4. They turn off the motor and sail with the wind.; 5. They have to decide who will take down the sails. Mr. Peterson takes down the sails.; 6. cold and fear; 7. Answers will vary.; 8. It was safe.; 9.–10. Answers will vary.

Page 64

1. B., clues: carry her belongings, hold many items, shoulder strap, match clothing; 2. C., clues: cool off and relax at the beach, leg opening; 3. B., clues: comfortable when standing all day, tried on

Page 65

1. C.–He answers phones, sits up front, greets visitors, and makes appointments.; 2. B.–She patrols her route and responds to calls about trouble.; 3. A.–He fixes problems in the building.; 4. C.–She has to get more information from the patient's owner.

Answer Key

Page 67

1. They poured cupfuls of hot water on it. Answers will vary.; 2.–4. Answers will vary.; 5. C; 6. A; 7. G; 8. D; 9. E; 10. B; 11. F

Page 68

Extra! Answers will vary.

Page 69

1. cause, effect; 2. effect, cause; 3. cause, effect; 4. cause, effect; 5. effect, cause; 6. cause, effect; 7. cause, effect; 8. effect, cause Extra! Answers will vary.

Page 71

1. bouquet; 2. flight; 3. Settlement; 4. dilapidated; 5. whinny; 6. tenement; 7. delivery; 8. tattered; 9. chatter; 10. laundry; 11. palace; 12. plush; 13. gorgeous; 14. spirit; 15. mending

Page 72

1. Then; 2. Both, 3. Both; 4. Both; 5. Now; 6. Then; 7. Both; 8. Then; 9. Both; 10. Both; 11. Both; 12. Both; 13. Both; 14. Both

Page 73

1. C.; 2. A.; 3. B.; 4. B.; 5. B.; 6. B.; 7. C.; 8. A.; Extra: Answers will vary.

Page 75

1. A.; 2. B.; 3. C.; 4. C.; 5. C.; 6. B.

Page 76

1. C.; 2. A.; 3. B.; 4. A.; 5. C.; 6. A.; 7. A.; 8. B.; 9. B.; 10. B.; Extra: sad

Page 77

1. B.; 2. A.; 3. A.; 4. B.; 5. B.; 6. A.; Extra: a watch

Page 78

1. effect, cause; 2. cause, effect; 3. effect, cause; 4. effect, cause; 5. effect, cause; 6. effect, cause; 7. effect, cause; 8. cause, effect; 9. cause, effect; Extra: The Mystery Society meets for the first time.

Page 80

1. cause, effect; 2. effect, cause; 3. effect, cause; 4. cause, effect; 5. effect, cause; 6. effect, cause; 7. cause, effect; Extra: a tree

Page 82

1. He wants a bike because all of his friends have one and riding one is faster than walking.; 2. His sister needs shoes and his grandfather is sick.; 3. He helps Mrs. Martinez, because she is an older woman with no one at home to help her.; 4. He gets a bike by doing the selfless, kind act of helping Mrs. Martinez.; Extra: Answers will vary.

Page 84

1. C; 2. train; 3. E, C; 4. Answers will vary.; 5. B; Extra: Answers will vary.

Page 86

1. C; 2. A; 3. B; 4. A; 5. B; 6. B; 7.–8. Answers will vary.

Page 87

A. 4, 3, 1, 5, 2; B. 5, 1, 3, 2, 4; C. 2, 4, 1, 5, 3; D. 3, 2, 5, 1, 4; 1. require, resist, reserve, represent; 2. hover, hound, hoop; 3. push, pulley, pudding, purple; 4. diesel, differ, digest, dictate

Page 88

1. invented, printing press; 2. Mount Rushmore; 3. invented, radio, phonograph; 4. ozone, environment; 5. clothing, late 1700s; 6. Mickey Mouse; 7. Harriet Tubman, Underground Railroad; 8. croquet; 9. climate, cactus; 10. function, liver; 11. animals, endangered, save; 12. foods, vitamin C; 13. Industrial Revolution, America; 14. political parties, England

Page 89

A. 1; B. 8; C. 6; D. 11; E. 1, 11; F. 9; G. 11, 5; H. 9; I. 6, 9; J. 7; K. 3, 12; L. 12; M. 10; N. 3; O. 9

Page 90

1. Jefferson City; 2. 8; 3. Nebraska, Kansas, Oklahoma; 4. St. Louis, Kansas City; 5. Mississippi River; 6. southwest; 7. St. Louis; 8. Kansas City; 9. Springfield; 10. Jefferson City

Page 91

1. *Trees in Your Backyard*; 2. *Washington, D. C.*; 3. *South American Countries*; 4. *Longitude and Latitude*; 5. *Competitive Team Sports*; 6. *U.S. State Capitals*; 7. *Organs of the Body*; 8. *Regions of the United States*; 9. *Famous Scientists*; 10. *American Indian Tribes*

Page 92

1. Chapter 5, pages 5, 12–18; 2. Chapter 1, pages 4–5; 3. Chapter 2, page 6; 4. Chapter 7, pages 20–22; 5. Chapter 6, page 19

Page 93

1. encyclopedia; 2. glossary; 3. atlas; 4. encyclopedia; 5. dictionary; 6. table of contents; 7. index; 8. atlas; 9. glossary; 10. encyclopedia